FACING

the

EXTREME

FACING

the

EXTREME

ONE WOMAN'S STORY OF
TRUE COURAGE, DEATH-DEFYING
SURVIVAL, AND HER QUEST
FOR THE SUMMIT

by RUTH ANNE KOCOUR
as told to MICHAEL HODGSON

St. Martin's Press ❧ *New York*

Design by Leah S. Carlson

ISBN 0-312-17942-1

First Edition: January 1998
10 9 8 7 6 5 4 3 2 1

For Jan ... May the mountain be the monument.

—*R.A.K*

For Nicole... Dream big, climb high.

—*DAD*

CONTENTS

AUTHOR'S NOTE

The story within these pages is true and is based on the personal journal I recorded during my climb of Denali in May 1992. Some of the conversations within the book have been re-created to the best of my recollection. The identities of Robert Link, head guide for Rainier Mountaineering, and Win Whittaker, assistant guide, have not been changed. However, I have intentionally changed the names of my seven male companions, without whom this climb would never have been possible (these names are denoted with an asterisk when they first appear). It is not for me to speak for them or tell their story. Each one of us had a unique experience on that mountain as we faced our own mortality, each armed with our individual, God-given resources. My account is only one person's perception, my own, and, in all fairness, my portraits of my teammates are necessarily incomplete since our only experience together was this one shared, horrendously trying event.

ACKNOWLEDGMENTS

While keeping journals of climbs and adventures has always been my habit, writing a book was the furthest thing from my mind. Illustrating books for others during my years as a medical illustrator convinced me that writing a book (not to mention getting it published) was an arduous "birthing" process—one I didn't need. So it was with considerable resistance that I responded to the urgings of friends and colleagues who wanted me to do so. Fortunately they were as persistent as I'm stubborn, and were it not for their interest, support, and encouragement, this book would not exist. Even the man at the dry cleaners told me it was important because "We all climb mountains in our minds." All of these influential people now deserve a heartfelt thank you.

Shortly after coming off Denali, I met Diane Strachan, who planted the seed for this project. She convinced me of the value in the experience—not only for me, but for others—and that the story needed to be told. She put me in touch with outdoor writer, Michael Hodgson, who had the vision to see this as a book worth writing and who demonstrated it with his skill, insight, wit, and the tenacity necessary to see it through. Without my co-author, Michael, this book would not exist. Best-selling author Beverly Whipple jumped in and shared with me her publishing experiences, mentored and spurred me on, and ultimately put me in contact with her literary agent, Heide Lange. Heide took the project and quickly made it reality. From there it was the enthusiasm and energy of our editor, Jennifer Enderlin at St. Martin's Press, and her publisher, Sally Richardson, who propelled the effort forward.

Others along the way lent their support and encouragement and helped retain my sanity. Barbara and Dick Fontaine sat in my kitchen and told me I really could write a book, and Randy and Judy Howatt insisted that a publisher could and would be found. Peter and Carol Read offered constant, quiet encouragement. Jenny Brouner listened patiently, followed every event graciously and attentively, and always said, "Ruth Anne, it *will* get published." Laurie Mola, Mary Helen Okeeffe, Donna DuCharme, and Cathy O'Brien each contributed their energy and inspiration, and Vickie Kahn offered to take charge of my wardrobe should I become famous. Carol Cone and Sally Edwards both provided professional advice and access to their vast lists of resources, which helped me move a little less blindly through the process.

And then there was Elizabeth Rassiga, Mary Ann Williams, Joanne Gipson, and Kate Crawford who, among other readers, shared their sage wisdom and honest criticisms. Elizabeth now claims I should have a warning label attached to my forehead that reads: "*Caution!* Knowing me could be hazardous to your health."

Bob, my wonderful husband, who's always said people should be allowed to live their dreams, has proven it with his unfailing love and support of my madcap undertakings. He openly claims to be a spoiled husband and is glad not to be sharing me any longer with the writing of a book—one he plans to read in the comfort of his hot tub—the same vantage point from which he climbs mountains (in his mind).

And finally I have to thank Peso, who, except for the occasional distraction of a squirrel, always led the way up the trail.

PREFACE

In May of 1992, during the worst storm on record to hit Mount McKinley, North America's highest peak at 20,320 feet, I and nine other teammates found ourselves clinging to the side of the mountain, fighting for survival instead of climbing toward the summit as we had hoped. Our struggle was eventually rewarded with a successful summit bid. Eleven other climber-mountaineers from other teams weren't so fortunate. They paid the ultimate price for their attempt to summit— death. "Inexperience," "bad luck," "bad weather," "their time," and "reckless bravado," are phrases that tattoo the memories and tagline the gravestones with more questions than answers. Four years later, same month, virtually the same time frame, disaster hit the mountaineering community again, this time on Everest. Eleven more gravestones, different names but etched with the same phrases ("inexperience," "bad luck," "bad weather," "their time," and "reckless bravado"), offer up what is a growing list of stark reminders to the risks inherent in mountaineering.

Climbing a mountain is always a calculated risk, a puppeteer's dance between heaven and hell where one false step, one miscalculation, one simple turn of fate, can leave a mountaineer tangled in a broken lifeline and tumbling into an icy coffin. Despite the obvious risks involved and the monumental failures of many, mountains such as McKinley compel the attentions of mountaineers around the world, drawing men and women in continuing record numbers rather like ants to a picnic. Why?

The Athabascan Indians call the continent's highest peak Denali, meaning "the High One" (I prefer this name and will use it throughout the book). It has been frequently referred to as the mountain of extremes and, more recently, the mountain of death. Rising above the tundra and piercing the heavens over central Alaska, Denali claims the most spectacular vertical gain of any point on earth. It has been characterized as a wilderness within a wilderness, looming alone amid a threatening and inhospitable landscape. Ice and snow blanket Denali year-round, while seven glaciers, hundreds of feet thick in places, carve immense valleys as they make their inexorable way down the mountain's sides. As the coldest and one of the most unforgiving places in the Northern Hemisphere, the physical environment of Denali ranks among the harshest on earth.

Because of its sheer mass, Denali begs to be explored, but like the allure of a female black widow to a male, the attraction is both seductive and deadly. High altitude, subarctic latitude, and notoriously severe weather combine to produce a world-class mountaineering challenge demanding fortitude, endurance, and skill. Mountaineers consistently underestimate Denali, and, particularly in ideal conditions, denial and self-deception can lull those who attempt the mountain into a dangerously false sense of security.

On Denali, sudden snowstorms can erupt out of nowhere, even in June, burying camps and trapping climbers in tents for days. Since the mountain itself can disappear behind a veil of clouds, air rescue becomes a chancy proposition. Even in good weather, mountaineers have lost their lives on Denali. Since 1932, when the National Park Service began keeping records, through 1996, eighty-seven climbers have perished in their quest for the summit. They died after being swept away by avalanches or by tumbling off rocky or icy walls. Some simply disappeared, swallowed by one of the many active glaciers that drape the mountain. Thirty-four of those who have died lie buried on the mountain, remembered only by line-item entries in Park Service logs as testament to their icy graves.

The compulsion to climb mountains has no logical explanation. In fact, there isn't anything that makes sense about mountaineering when taken at face value. Where is the attraction in spending a month of your life struggling to reach the rarefied air and glory of a mountain's summit, only to spin around abruptly after a mere ten minutes or so to race back to the safety of a lower camp?

Jim Whittaker, the first American to summit Everest, once said that mountaineering "is like hitting oneself in the head with a hammer—it only feels good when you stop." Others have referred to climbing successfully as nothing more than one's measured ability to endure pain. Since Denali, I've begun referring to mountaineering as "crisis reduced to a mental exercise."

Fortunately, mountaineering is seldom the arduous experience we endured on Denali or the disaster of monumental proportions experienced in 1996 on Everest. If it were, we would have to stop referring to it as a sport and instead dub the pursuit of mountaineering as something similar to a suicide mission. At its best, high-elevation mountaineering offers accomplishment for the sake of growth as well as sport without competition where the concept of winning doesn't necessarily mean coming in first. The mountain becomes the means to improve the person, which works so long as the person involved doesn't have deluded ideas about "conquering" the mountain.

I'm compelled to climb mountains for a number of reasons. As an artist, I climb for the visual feast. Visuals absolutely turn me on—the light, the perspectives, the Jules Verne otherworldliness of the mountainscape, the intensity of the colors, the massive scale, the shadow of the earth cast against its own atmosphere. There is, quite simply, nothing on earth that matches the visuals from a mountain summit and, to me, any hardship or discomfort is well worth the privilege of being there. Of course, friends have taken great delight in pointing out the dichotomy between using my hands for the delicate and precise work as a medical illustrator and using them for the blue-collar, muscle-wrenching work of climbing. While I can't debate the obvious contrast of efforts between my two passions, they share a similar need for intense concentration and attention to detail—something I absolutely revel in.

I climb because challenging situations thrill me. I delight in finding order in chaos—perhaps the result of being the oldest of six children. I've been told I'm a type A personality gone wild. I'm most at ease in a situation that demands my complete focus and forces me to push my limits. For some reason, the harder things become, the more I like doing them—perhaps a dysfunctional soul is requisite to being a successful mountaineer?

I climb, too, because I truly love being in the vertical environment—I'm at home there, totally at ease—and because the high alpine world is a source of endless fascination that energizes and makes me feel more alive than at any other time in my life. I dream about mountaineering. It's in my blood and I dread the thought of a day when I might be physically unable to do it.

Mountaineering is a "white-hot imperative"—that single interest in life that motivates me in everything else that I do. On a mountain, I find that I am able to peel away the camouflage under which all humans hide and experience existence in a pure state, stripped to the bare essentials—life in the raw with its flaws and beating heart exposed for all to see. It is this baring of one's soul that leads to personal awareness and the feeling that one is truly alive. What is also fascinating to me is being a part of the natural process of evolution that all teams go through when under stress. Strength or weakness in a team is derived directly from human ability to deal with fear and challenges, and builds character as a result. Members of every climbing team I've ever been on have managed to gel only as each person managed to understand and accept idiosyncratic behavior in others. Personalities are neither bad nor good when on the mountain, although from the outside looking in, as you the reader are now, that can be hard to see. The challenge of learning to work together is a challenge as great as climbing the summit itself.

As for dealing with the risks, I simply never think that I'm risking my life when I head off on a climb, and I refuse to operate from that perspective. Even on Denali, where the very weight of the mountain's force had crushed the last breath out of so many other climbers before, I didn't set out with the thought that I was risking my life. I am more afraid of not living than I am of dying. My goal was to experience what Dick Bass had described to me years earlier as "the most spectacular of the

Seven Summits." The Seven Summits represent the highest point on each of the seven continents and a lofty goal millionaire Bass popularized in his quest to be the first to climb them all. The Seven Summits are Mount Kosciusko in Australia (7,316 feet); Mount Aconcagua in South America (22,834 feet); Mount Kilimanjaro in Africa (19,340 feet); Denali in North America (20,320 feet); Mount Elbrus in Europe (18,482 feet); Mount Vinson in Antarctica (16,864 feet); and Mount Everest in Asia (29,028 feet). Before Denali, I had climbed Elbrus, Kilimanjaro, and Aconcagua. For many, Denali is more than just another box to tick off on the Seven Summit checklist. It is a coveted jewel that sparkles in the eyes of mountaineers who would ascend to the lofty heights of world-class mountaineering. Those who make it revel in the throne rooms of the mountain gods. Those who don't, either keep trying until they succeed or end their attempt by choice or force. I had been dreaming of Denali's summit for years.

For most of my mountaineering life, the mountains have been good to me. Yes, I acknowledge that climbing in a world of fire and ice is a carefully choreographed dance in a hostile environment, one I've always had tremendous respect for— certainly more so after my experience on Denali. But, without actually experiencing what I went through on the mountain in May 1992, I could never have imagined or even appreciated the magnitude of the forces of life and death that swirl within the mountain zone.

When the climb up Denali began to turn deadly, it might seem surprising to others to hear that I was able to numb myself to the icy tendrils of terror that threatened to choke the life from any unwary soul. Probably this was because the experience was not a fast, intense, adrenaline rush. Instead, my teammates and I were forced to live with a closeness of death for so many days that death itself became familiar, almost comfortable. My experience on Denali bestowed on me a familiarity with death. I knew its face, its habits, its haunts. With that knowledge comes an incredible sense of freedom (though not recklessness) that now allows me to move through many aspects of life, including my continued pursuit of mountains, unencumbered. Living with death has taught me to stay in the moment, fully focused and aware, without fear of the future—to me, a far more enriching approach to life.

A friend once told me that the only people who ever reach the top of any mountain, metaphorical or real, are those who have experienced intense pain. Everyone has tasted life's hard blows at some point in time. How those blows are dealt with determines whether or not the experience becomes constructive or destructive. The more I climbed real mountains, I discovered that I had allowed past blows—unresolved issues in my life—to fester as pent-up anger. I learned to harness this anger as energy, energy that drove me to great heights, literally. After Denali, I realized I had no more anger left. This mountain took it all from me—Denali was bigger than any anger I could possibly harbor.

Is the struggle and the risk of death worth those ten minutes on the summit? If you take those ten minutes alone and strip away all else, probably not.

To paraphrase T. S. Eliot, no matter how much time I spend exploring faraway places, the result will be to end up where I started, at the beginning, seeing my life with new understanding. That, for me, sums up the worth of the pursuit of rarefied air and mountain summits. As hard as the experience gets, it's never just the summit. It's each step along the way and the sights seen and the lessons learned that make the ten minutes on the summit so special. Yet even without the summit, other, "internal" summits are climbed, so in many ways, mountaineering is, for me, more about the journey than anything else. This meaning is perfectly described by a Zen saying: "The journey is the end."

Though I didn't know it on May 1, 1992, the greatest journey of my life was about to begin. If Denali had a doorman, he might well say, "Welcome to Denali, where your nightmares and dreams commingle in an often confused sense of reality."

{1} ON THE ROAD TO DENALI

It is hard to celebrate life when one is surrounded by death, imprisoned by a raging storm on the side of a mountain that some assert is the most dangerous summit in the world. I had intended the climb to be a forty-fifth birthday present, but this was no gift. I was an unwilling participant in my worst nightmare. A member of a nearby climbing team went outside simply to dig out his tent and when he returned and took a sip of hot cocoa, his teeth cracked. Even unexposed skin was turning yellow-and-black—freezing, dying. The wind roaring down the mountain and thundering by our tents sounded like passing freight trains, the avalanches like bombs. The ground shook from the ferocity of it all. I had to wear earplugs just to muffle the noise. Body bags stacked around the medical tent became final resting places for those who were now beyond help. I'd look at one and wonder: Why not me? Why not all of us? *Living and dying had been reduced to a simple game of roulette that played on with no end in sight.*

If I only knew then what I know now...

I looked ridiculous! A passing hiker, wearing a small fanny pack and dressed in shorts, a T-shirt, and lightweight hiking shoes, managed to nod a greeting despite his obvious inclination to stare at the strange, six-foot-tall, blue-eyed blonde who strode by—running tights, sweatshirt, bandanna, dark glasses, an expedition pack loaded until the seams strained, ski poles, and giant plastic expedition boots with heavy socks stretched to mid-calf. I had to agree that it was a ridiculous getup for a dayhike in Reno, Nevada's, 70-degree weather with not a single snowflake in sight. In two days I would board a flight from Reno to Seattle and then on to Anchorage where I would meet up with my teammates for the first time. Barring bad weather or any other unforeseen challenges, in three days I would be sitting in a camp alongside a makeshift glacial airstrip at Kahiltna Base at 7,200 feet—13,120 feet below the summit of my dreams. Today, however, I walked. One final training hike along familiar Sierra paths with my dog, Peso. At least he never cared how strange I appeared. Of course, that was probably due in large part to Peso's own unique visual presentation.

Peso, the end result of generations of random procreation, confounded even the veterinarian, rendering him unable to pinpoint a single contributing breed. Peso mystified everyone. He sported the fur of a chow, the legs of a basset hound, and a head suggesting a hint of German shepherd somewhere in his genealogy. As he would prance happily up to strangers on the trail, they would smile and in turn wonder aloud: "Was he exotic?" "What happened to his legs?" "Is he a normal dog standing in a hole?" or "Was he the result of a dog being dropped from a very high building?" Only one thing ever remained certain. Peso was unique.

He earned his name the moment I paid $10 for him as a pup, taking him off the hands of two Mexican children in Reno. A scrawny little mutt, he didn't look as if he were worth much more than a peso and, since he came from a Mexican family, the name stuck. Today I wouldn't sell him for a million pesos. Peso has become my most loyal and loving trail companion. As I watched him bounce and weave up the trail now, his little paws kicking up tiny puffs of dust as he ran, my mind began to drift, tracing the days and years that had led me here and that now pointed toward a distant summit.

An artist by profession and a climber by choice, high-elevation mountaineering offered another medium for approaching life in a positive way. My focus over the years of mountaineering, skiing, and technical rock- and ice-climbing, had evolved gradually from a simple interest in physical fitness to a more sophisticated fascination with human limits, especially my own. I began to use the mountains as my personal alpine laboratory, adopting a systematic approach to testing myself and my stamina, both physically and mentally. The objective on each climb was to reach and perhaps even surpass my own boundaries of excellence, but not by measuring myself against others. This was about me and no one else.

To this day my hands bear the scars of years devoted to rock climbing. Gertz Uhrsler, a tall, tan, well-built, blue-eyed, then twenty-six-year-old German-Swiss alpinist with white blond hair, introduced me to the sport in Boulder, Colorado, during the spring of 1967. A former guide in the Alps, he found joy in daily shepherding me up many of the most difficult ascents the nearby Flat Irons and canyons could offer. He taught me to pattern myself after technically expert climbers and encouraged me to place myself in their company in order that I might be pushed to achieve the highest level of climbing excellence possible. We were inseparable for nearly two years.

It was also Gertz who made me painfully aware of the potential hazards of mountaineering, though not intentionally. He returned to Switzerland to guide for the summer in 1969. On a routine ascent of the Matterhorn, while anchoring his team of four, the lead person slipped, popping out a badly placed piton. His fall yanked the next two on the rope off the face. Gertz managed to hold the entire group for fifteen seconds before being pulled to his death by the overwhelming weight. I had lost a childhood friend the year before, to a non-climbing-related accident, and to now have to face the young death of Gertz impacted me profoundly. Death was now part of my reality.

I drifted from the world of climbing and climbers as I embarked on a professional career (the toll climbing placed on my hands was not good for my performance at the drawing table), but the mountains were never very far from my soul. Extreme skiing replaced climbing and became the recreational and emotional escape of my adult life. Snow became the medium upon which I could push the boundaries, reaching ever further and further into the recesses of my mind and body to discover abilities and overcome fears I'd never imagined.

I was pulled back to the lures of ascending in a vertical world by an invitation to climb Mount Kilimanjaro in 1986 with Peter Whittaker, a world-class alpinist from a legendary mountaineering family. Though going down mountains has its attraction, it was the going up that I missed, so I leapt at the chance. I never had a burning desire for high peaks, but Kilimanjaro was as good an excuse as any to see Africa and get in a bit of climbing at the same time.

Kilimanjaro, at 19,340 feet, is a vast, extinct volcano that towers above Africa as that continent's highest peak. Its crater spans six miles and although it is not a technically difficult mountain to climb, its enormity makes the trek both physically and emotionally memorable.

Beginning at 6,000 feet, our team, led by a Tanzanian guide with two club feet and only one eye, spent five days working our way up the Machame route, arriving at first light on the morning of the fifth day. Glaciers, which still clung tenuously to the sides of the crater rim and stood nearly thirty stories high, began to reflect the bright pink luminescence of the alpenglow. This combined with the bright red of the volcanic rock and the enormity of the crater and its six-mile span left me feeling as if I were standing on Mars. I watched the sun as it rose into the African sky, gently tracing its fingers of light across the entire floor of Tanzania far below.

This sudden insight into the mystical pull and attraction of climbing mountains left me dangling between worlds of exhilaration and exasperation. Thrilled that I now had a clear sense of what I wanted to pursue, I was frustrated that I had discovered this sport so late in life. I had always rejected the axiom that positioned aging as an inevitable degenerative disease, but now the possibility that my aging might prevent my experiencing the mountains as I wanted gnawed at me.

To my great relief, my friend Jim Whittaker cited age as a distinct advantage. He noted that younger climbers often allow brute strength to supersede correct climbing methods and techniques. Listing many well-known mountaineers—all in their mid-forties—he credited technical prowess and wisdom as the keys to their efficiency.

His remarks called to mind an account I had heard about

Peruvian Indian couriers known for running at very high altitudes. Researchers, hearing that these runners were not youths, but rather advanced in age, went to investigate. The scientists confirmed that young boys were indeed outperformed by older men, with the strongest of the runners ranking as senior citizens. It seems that the Indian culture taught that experience and knowledge accumulated over the years translated into greater performance. Challenging the commonly accepted paradigm of aging, the message rang clear. We become the product of our expectations.

What I saw in Jim Whittaker translated into an energetic, fit young man of sixty who still organized and led climbing expeditions around the globe. Buoyed by this revelation, I practically floated back home. My time to summit the distant peaks of this world had arrived.

It was in 1987, while climbing on Orizaba, the second-highest point in North America at 18,701 feet, that I learned to turn inward, into what Zen masters refer to as "creating the perfect mental state." Because of the duration of the climb, the slow, rhythmic pace, and the utilization of a high-altitude breathing technique known as "pressure breathing," I lapsed into a very efficient and almost hypnotic mode of movement. It afforded my first exposure to performance without conscious effort, and as a result, despite forty-mile-per-hour winds and a chill factor of minus twenty degrees Fahrenheit, the climb seemed easy.

My next big mountain, during 1988 in between home-based ice-climbing training, was Mount Elbrus in the former U.S.S.R. The mountain was neither technically demanding nor difficult, and at a mere 18,510 feet, I had already been higher. The eye-opener for me centered around the grim realities of Communism, which exceeded my wildest dreams. The trip and climb became more about surviving the state of the Soviet Union than surviving the mountain.

Pete, still my mountaineering mentor and actively managing my progression up the mountaineering-skills ladder, picked Aconcagua as my next test, in 1990. Aconcagua, located in South America, is the tallest mountain in the Western Hemisphere at 22,834 feet, and the second-highest of the Seven Summits. This mountain would also serve as my official indoctrination into the world of really dangerous mountains. It has been said that Aconcagua kills more people than any other mountain in the world.

Standing in a crowded Argentine government office in Mendoza, waiting to get our climbing permit, I was struck by the almost overwhelming lack of preparedness exhibited by many of these would-be mountaineers: out of shape, antiquated equipment, false bravado, and, in many instances, absolutely no clue regarding their surroundings or the seriousness represented by undertaking a summit attempt on such an exposed and high peak. I was beginning to gain insight into why so many died on this mountain—it's too damn accessible for too many inexperienced people. There is no higher point between the Pacific Ocean and Aconcagua. Consequently, storms slam into the mountain with unrelenting fury and amazing speed. One minute it can be clear and calm and the next minute winds as high as 100 miles per hour will roar in and attempt to tear the unsuspecting and unprepared from the mountain or bury them under a blinding blizzard of snow.

Our team, though, was the picture of invincibility. Mark Tucker, another RMI (Rainier Mountaineering) guide along with Pete, was here training for an upcoming Everest attempt. He would be going along with Jim Whittaker on Whittaker's now famous 1990 peace climb. But it wasn't his mountaineering experience that intrigued me. It was the fact that people kept referring to him as "the man who ate his way out of a tent."

When I pressed him for an explanation, he obliged. While camped with his partner Robert Link during an attempt on Denali the year before, he had felt a weight suddenly pressing the tent down onto his back. Realizing that they were victims of an avalanche, Mark reacted quickly and instinctively rolled over and put his arms above his face to create an air space. Using his teeth to gnaw and tear at the tent's fabric he literally ate his way out of the tent and then clawed his way to the snow's surface. Their entire camp had been obliterated. Mark first rescued Robert and then proceeded to dig out eight other climbers, saving everyone—this in temperatures of 7 degrees Fahrenheit, wearing only his long underwear and socks and digging with bare hands.

It was also on Aconcagua that I experienced for the first time the chaos of a big mountain basecamp. Over two hundred aspiring climbers perched together on a jumble of rocks at 13,700 feet, all acclimatizing and waiting for the moment to arrive when they could stop swapping tales of success and failure and begin an assault on the mountain. From above, the tent city took on a surreal Technicolor display that dotted the landscape. High-tech, low-tech, and no-tech—it was all here.

One enterprising local had set up a concession tent, complete with a billboard that read:

SERVICES

Mountain Guide
Porter
Hire Mule
Rescue Service
Breakfast
Beer
Hot Dog
Hamburger
Take Care Equipment

The "Take Care Equipment" was perhaps his most enter-prising venture (read, "Extortion"). Your equipment was safe so long as you paid the service fee. If you elected to forgo his pro-tection, things would begin disappearing. One team, fortunately finished with their climbing, had all their boots stolen, leaving them with no choice but to hike out the thirty miles to the road in stocking feet. Our first night, a pair of trekking boots was stolen from outside our tent. A sleeping bag also managed to "disappear" overnight from another team's tent—a significant threat to survival. You only have to beat your head against a wall for so long before you realize that by stopping, the pain goes away. So convinced, we accepted our "insurance broker's" offer of protection.

Stories of horror on the mountain began to filter my way, many of them via a young Australian lad who claimed to be a survivor of brain surgery and was now on Aconcagua with his "mate" trying to set a world record for climbing from basecamp to the summit—10,000 vertical feet in seven hours. A week later, it would take us all of seven hours just to go from our high camp at 19,700 feet to the summit. His companion, a veteran speed climber, already held the record for scaling Everest from basecamp to summit: sixteen hours. During their three weeks on Aconcagua, they had managed to reach the summit seven times, and in the course of their yo-yoing up and down the mountain, they had taken part in more than their fair share of rescues.

It was through his eyes that I began to get a glimpse into the Western world's perception of Asian mountaineers. This perception, which became firsthand experience for me when on Denali, is perhaps somewhat of an unfair generalization since there are some superb Japanese and Korean climbers. It is, however, a view that has its roots firmly planted in the reality of common mountaineering experiences—nearly everyone who has mountaineered for any length of time has been witness to Asian team disasters.

According to my newfound Aussie friend, they had been coming off the summit and were at 21,000 feet when they passed a team of three Japanese climbers, two men and one woman. The two men were in front of the woman by approximately one hundred feet when she simply dropped to the ground in a heap. The two men turned and saw her drop but continued on their way to the summit, leaving their companion like a pile of unnecessary equipment that would only slow their summit attempt should they have to carry it. One of the Australians who saw this happen ran back up to one of the Japanese men, forcefully spun him around, and pointed at the woman. The man refused to have anything to do with her and continued on to the summit, leaving the Aussies to deal with the situation. They carried her down to their high camp (Berlin Camp) at 19,700 feet, gave her some oxygen, and then ferried her all the way down to 13,700 feet and basecamp where she could receive vital medical attention. It turned out that she had both cerebral and pulmonary edemas. The Aussies never found out if she survived.

Two other Japanese climbers had arrived days before in the basecamp and spent the night sucking down oxygen from a canister instead of trying to acclimatize. The following morning, they set off at a brisk pace toward the summit and were discovered by the Australians later that day wandering aimlessly around Berlin Camp, completely incoherent. Although they had just hiked up themselves, the Aussies had no choice but to short-rope (several feet of tight rope to act as a kind of leash) these two and lead them quickly off the mountain and to the safety of basecamp.

Referencing Denali, a favorite climbing destination for the Asian mountaineering community, the Aussies surmised that Asians commonly got into so much trouble because they were generally in a hurry, making it inevitable that many would fall prey to this blinders-on, "the summit is the only important thing" mentality that drives them upward.

This is not to imply that the Asians had a lock on lunacy or simple misfortune on Aconcagua, or any other mountain for that matter. Several Floridians and one German had to be evacuated by the Aussies because they were in over their heads, too. Another climber died after reaching the high glacier simply because he forgot his crampons (metal claws, designed to provide grip and traction on icy surfaces, that strap to the bottom of one's boots and resemble something you'd find in a medieval torture chamber), and elected to continue climbing instead of turning back, by chopping steps up the mountain. The method worked well until he slipped.

Blown retinas, various stages of altitude sickness, heart attacks, intestinal disorders of the worst kind, and even kidneys that shut down, causing the victim to urinate blood (an acute condition brought on by a failure to drink sufficiently at altitude)—these are the challenges that meet doctors who fortunately populate basecamp, presenting a visual image that at times more resembles a M.A.S.H. unit than a mountaineering staging point.

By far the most insidious and dangerous of the maladies to strike anyone at altitude is a pulmonary or cerebral edema. Pulmonary edema, an acute symptom of altitude also known as "dry-land drowning," develops when the capillaries in the lungs rupture, leaving the victim drowning in his own froth of blood. Cerebral edema, a swelling of the brain induced by elevation, causes headaches at first, and in extreme cases can become fatal. I credit my high tolerance for altitude to a small brain allowing adequate room for expansion. Intelligence never has been a prerequisite for mountaineering!

Far from a preoccupation with the macabre aspects of the mountaineering experience, hearing of other's misfortunes dramatized for me the importance of good planning and decisions, proper acclimatization and highly qualified guides. Being on Aconcagua also taught me that despite all the best-laid plans, the presence of other teams could and would impact us, and their inexperience or carelessness could become our undoing if we did not stay on our toes.

All the way to the summit, we dodged horrendous rockfalls,

triggered most often by the thoughtless actions of climbing teams above. One rockslide swept right through a place where our tents had been pitched only hours before. During the final push for the peak, we were working our way up a narrow chute, directly below a French team. The periodic shower of rocks that would glance by caused Peter to summon all of us over to the protected side of the chute to wait out the "idiots" above. Just as we reached safety, the leader triggered a monumental rockslide that began raining rocks and even boulders upon his own team below. All I could do was watch in horror and listen to the awful sound of rock grinding against rock as a dining-room-table–sized boulder blasted into the last member of the French team, hurling him to the ground as it bounced by. As we debated whether we should head out there to retrieve the body, the unfortunate soul sat upright. Luckily, the impact had only broken his glasses and left a few cuts and bruises he would no doubt feel the next day. The resulting adrenaline rush left my heart pounding to such an extent I thought I was on the verge of a heart attack. The experience left me so exhausted it was almost more than I could recover from, though recover I did. I made another mental note to myself—learn to control my emotions because a successful mountaineer cannot afford the energy drain of that rush.

The final memory I would take with me to Denali came after we had left the summit. While on top of Aconcagua, we noticed a storm roaring in from the west and it looked like it was going to be a classic howler. That storm chased us all the way off the mountain, motivating us in such a way that we made it all the way out to the road in only three days instead of the usual five. It wasn't until later that I heard the storm we raced to escape had left nine dead in its wake as it ripped across Aconcagua. Mountains can be merciless.

Later in 1990, Peter suggested that he would like me to join him on a climb in fall 1993 up Everest. I readily accepted and signed on to a prerequisite 1992 Denali trip being led by Robert Link and Win Whittaker. Because of its fierce weather reputation, altitude, and level of mountaineering difficulty, both psychologically and physically, Denali is generally considered a "must-do" mountain before graduation to the really serious mountains in the Himalayas.

Denali! A forty-fifth birthday present to myself. Peso skidded by me on an urgent mission to who-knows-where, bringing my thoughts back to home base. Two days and I would be on my way.

Sitting in the hot tub that night, sharing a last moment with my husband, Bob, before departure, I stared up at the million pinpricks of light that danced and twinkled against the backdrop of an inky black Sierra sky. Far from feeling abandoned during my adventures, Bob headed off to enjoy his own—this time windsurfing in Hawaii. My first choice would have been to share the mountains I climbed with Bob, but he wanted nothing to do with it, calling the experience "an endeavor that sounds grimy and unpleasant." Bob has even gone so far as to define his personal boundaries of climbing as "any hike which concludes in my hot tub," and happily offers this definition of mountaineering to anyone who cares to listen: "a massive headache with no hope of sex."

Following Kilimanjaro, Bob did confess that he had taken my being home for granted all those years and extolled the positive impact of my African excursion on our relationship, although his views on climbing had not been altered.

"Sweetheart, I want you to feel comfortable leaving home to climb any mountain in the world that you desire, just so long as you never try to make me go, too."

Now happily married for twenty years, I've been leaving him ever since.

A shooting star flashed across the sky, taking me with it and toward the summit of Denali.

Bob gently squeezed my arm, pulling me back from my brief mental sojourn.

"You're already on the mountain, aren't you?" he conjectured.

I smiled and kissed him. My best friend—the man knows me well.

It was May 1, 1992, the day following the worst riots to rock the country in a decade—riots ignited by the acquittal of Los Angeles police officers charged in the beating of a black motorist. Violence threatened to erupt as far north as Seattle as I followed the news coverage while connecting through airports. The timing seemed perfect for a trip to Alaska.

The mountaineering season on Denali runs from May 1 to

August 1. By climbing early we would encounter fewer people, more secure snow bridges on which to cross crevasses and, theoretically, better weather as we advanced up the mountain.

The piles of baggage, duffels, and packs just outside the baggage claim area marked our group's arrival and meeting point at the International Airport in Anchorage. I was the last to arrive, so introductions were of the brief, name-only variety: lead guide Robert Link, assistant guide Win Whittaker, and teammates Franklin*, John*, Paul*, Randy*, Vern*, Craig*, and Jack*.

Following the intros, we were herded out to the passenger pickup point. I had been so excited about the prospects of climbing with all the modern conveniences common to a "First World" country; then I was introduced to what Robert referred to as the "Denali overland transport," a decidedly dilapidated piece of machinery of undetermined age and make that only loosely met the legal definitions of "vehicle." Parked alongside the curb, our official transport, in a former life, may have served its passengers well as a minischoolbus. Its current incarnation, complete with bald tires, springs that shrieked and complained as we unloaded gear, and a coat of dingy, peeling gray paint, did not inspire confidence. I began to wonder if it might not be quicker, and certainly safer, to hire a mule to get us to Talkeetna.

The hood was already up when we arrived and the driver seemed intent on concluding his negotiations with "the four-wheeled sumnabitch" with either verbal abuse or physical violence. So far, so normal—every mountaineering trip I had ever been on, albeit ones in Third World countries, had begun with vehicle failures. Why should this be any different just because we were in the good ol' U.S. of A.? After an hour of cajoling, the engine was finally coaxed to turn over and sputter to life, and we began a very jumpy and bumpy seventy-mile journey to Talkeetna.

Robert plopped down next to the driver. At thirty-four, he had been on eight trips to Denali, summiting five times. He had also been to Everest three times, summiting it once in 1990 as the leader of Jim Whittaker's International Peace climb. He was born into the mountaineering life with a father who was a soldier in the 10th Mountain Division made famous in World War II. Robert had spent his entire life guiding and knew no other way to make a living. He was short (5 feet 8 inches) but powerful, sporting just a hint of a belly he swore he'd lose on the mountain. His smile flashed white against his dark skin and black, thick beard. It was Robert's reputation as a leader and mountaineer, coupled with my desire to climb with him, that had brought me here.

Aside from Robert, Win was the only other team member I knew and the only one I had actually climbed with, having ascended Rainier with both him and his brother Peter previously. So thin you could almost see right through him, Win was mature beyond his twenty-six years. This was his first return to the mountain since leaving guiding a while back to pursue a career in music—apparently an attempt to establish an identity separate from that of his famous mountaineering family.

A quick survey of the vital statistics of our crew revealed an age range from twenty-six to forty-five, with me holding the senior position. In this case, age served me well, translating into experience and positioning me as the most seasoned mountaineer outside of Robert and Win. Already there was a lot of talk among the others, a banter of bravado that began to border on excessive. It was going to be interesting to see where all the talk would lead once we were on the mountain. I turned to a window and gazed at trees, meadows, and cabins slipping by, while the whine of tire rubber on the Alaska highway sang a hypnotic serenade.

Fortunately, Talkeetna sits perched at the end of a spur road that juts northeast from the Alaska Highway. Fortunate, because if it did not sit at the end of a road, drivers might roar right by even as they were applying their brakes. Only two blocks long, Talkeetna boasts only one paved road, but one bar for every household, or so it seems. There are times, I've heard, when the Harleys and mutts appear to outnumber the humans. Over one of the three public telephones in town, someone had pinned a single sheet torn from a phone book—it represented the entire population. Most of the buildings had outhouses behind them and a town sign proudly boasted that Talkeetna was home to the annual "Moose Dropping Festival." Being proud of an animal's droppings and building a festival around it struck me as a bit strange, but then, that also speaks to the humorous and somewhat renegade spirit that courses through the blood of every resident in town. Talkeetna is also home to a ragtag collection of highly skilled bush pilots who spend their lives, however long or short, shuttling mountaineers, gear, sightseers, mail, and anything else you might imagine, into places so wild and rugged no one in their right mind would attempt to fly, let alone land. Talkeetna is a throwback to the days of the Wild West, and the bush pilots are its resident hired guns.

The roadside sign announced the Talkeetna Motel, our lodging for the next two nights. Directions were simple: AT END OF PAVEMENT. An A-frame building still adorned with Christmas lights served as the motel's bar and registration desk. The screen door leading to the back and our rooms had no screen, but we opened it anyway out of respect for its effort to appear like a real door. The yard between the office-cum-bar and the motel itself was filled with chained dogs, abandoned cars, and a number of Harley-Davidsons. I had been told my room was located "down the hallway to the second door on the right." The hallway amounted to nothing more than a path that ran under the plywood-covered space between two long trailers parked lengthwise and side-by-side. I discovered the door to my room after worming my way around a pile of odds and ends that concealed the entrance. At six feet by twelve feet, my abode was more of a roomlet, with aspirations of becoming a real room when it grew up. It did have a great bathroom, though, so I really couldn't complain. Compared to the upcoming confines of a tent and the exposure of dropping pants before God and country, this was an absolute palace.

Talkeetna is 250 miles from Denali and the closest point of civilization for those, like us, seeking to gain its summit. Sitting almost at sea level, Talkeetna was a balmy 35 degrees Fahrenheit, but word reached our group as we unloaded at the motel that temperatures were hovering at a chilly minus-20 degrees Fahrenheit at basecamp, nearly 7,000 feet above where we now stood.

Not quite ready for the official fifteen-minute tour of town, we wandered back to the motel's office and bellied up to the bar. I struck up a conversation with Sally, the waitress, who had come to Alaska as a young bride with her husband. There was a simple and pleasant openness about her. The bartender, a rather fat and elderly gentleman, had apparently been listening to my conversation with Sally because he sidled over and, looking at me out of the corner of his eyes, began a line of interrogation.

"Aren't many women who climb this mountain, missy. Ya ever done this kind of thing before?"

I nodded. "Yes, I've climbed mountains all over the world."

"Well, let me tell you. You're in for one helluva surprise. This ain't any ordinary mountain. It's not like the others."

"Oh? So then you've climbed Denali yourself, have you?" Judging by his shape, this wasn't likely, but the question flattered him nonetheless.

"Nope. Don't ever intend to, either. Heard too many stories, seen too many things. My boy, he climbed it a while back. Only a loaf of bread with him . . . had a helluva time."

My eyes opened wide in mock surprise: "You sure it was Denali he climbed?"

"Yep, sure was," he said, toweling off the top of the bar.

Struggling to keep a straight face, I lifted my glass of tonic-and-lime as a toast and managed a fairly sincere "Really. Wow. That's quite an accomplishment."

"He's quite a boy. You the only woman in this group?"

I nodded.

"Soooo, do ya like that?" He was leaning into the bar, leering at me.

Though I had the urge to knock him silly, I resisted and offered what I thought was as civil an answer as he deserved:

"I really don't think about it. I love the sport, and there aren't many women who do. So, I like to go with men."

"I'll bet you do. How do *they* feel about having a woman along?" he said, leaning even more in my direction while stroking his chin with his hand.

"So far it has never been an issue and I don't intend to make it one," I replied firmly, looking straight into his eyes.

I wondered if I had passed the pop quiz as he shuffled back down the bar, shaking his head. The mountain is not the place to draw gender distinctions, though this was not the first time I had faced down a Spanish inquisition. I choose not to focus on the fact that I am a woman and because I don't, others rarely do—thank goodness.

Chugging down the last of my tonic-and-lime, I bade my comrades good night and headed back to my cubicle for a peaceful night's rest. I had a feeling I was going to need it.

{2} DANCING WITH STRANGERS

SATURDAY, MAY 2

Sun filtering through the dusty window in my roomlet announced the morning. There was no point in trying to sleep any longer, so despite the hour—five A.M.—I slid out of bed. I spent the next five minutes trying to keep from knocking myself senseless since my head had a tendency to bump the walls each time I bent over to pull on another article of clothing.

I made my way outside and onto Main Street. All was still. Even the dogs weren't barking. It was a perfect time to call Bob.

"Morning, sweetheart, it's me from sunny Talkeetna."

"Morning, lover. Boy I miss you. How's the team?"

"They seem really nice. . . . Time will tell. A couple of 'em talk way too much, but I guess that's just because they're a bit rattled. I think my tentmate, Craig, will be really great, though. He's a paramedic—very solid, and appears very levelheaded."

"If you get in a car accident you're in good hands, then?" My husband, the humorist.

"The weather? Does it look okay?" His tone had changed.

"It's clear and cold, minus-twenty on the mountain, thirty here in town. It's really, really good, almost too good. I know it's got to change sometime, but we're so well equipped that there won't be any problems."

"Well . . . you know I'll be sending warm thoughts your way every day, honey."

"I'm counting on that. I've gotta go. I need some breakfast before we start sorting gear in the hangar."

"Good-bye, lover. . . . You be extra careful."

"Always am. I love you."

My fingers traced a line down the handset as my mind reached to touch the man on the other end. A slight breeze cut through the stillness, stirring a chorus of barks that punctuated the end of what had been an idyllic morning.

The growl in my stomach reminded me of the immediate need for food. No one else from the team was up yet, so I breakfasted alone in the Talkeetna Motel. Feeling bold, I ordered reindeer sausages along with my eggs, biscuits, and orange juice. I was a little disappointed when they arrived looking like any other sausage patty, although I'm not sure how else they should have appeared—wearing tiny antlers perhaps?

Craig plopped down just as I was dusting off my final biscuit and chasing away the strong, gamy taste of reindeer with a swig of juice.

"Morning, Ruth Anne. Sleep well?"

"Yes, and you?"

"Not enough. We ended up at the Fairview Inn for a few final drinks. Whadda place!"

I had some idea what he was talking about. The night before, I'd poked my head into the open front door just to check out the scene. Not a drinker, I had no intention of staying, despite the Welcome sign. What I saw convinced me that the Fairview, Talkeetna's only all-night bar, was no place for a

woman. The music reverberated so loudly it shook every inch
of the white two-story, wood-sided building—they probably had
to replace nails and the odd window or two with regularity. A
bar ran the length of the room, and reindeer heads, antlers, skins,
caribou racks, and hundreds of black-and-white photos of Alaskan old-timers adorned every spare inch of wall space not filled
with bottles. Tap beer, whiskey, and "Denali daiquiris" were the
beverages of choice. The minute I entered, every male eye in the
place fixed on me, speeding my retreat, but not before noticing
that the wide-open front door was mirrored by a wide-open back
door.

"So you had a wild time, then?"

"You're not going to believe this, but while we were sitting
there sipping a draft, a couple of guys on motorcycles rode right
through the front door and then right out the back."

Now I understood the open doors. I sat for a while longer
to keep Craig company until the rest of the team arrived. He
had a solid, athletic appearance. At five foot nine, with a thin
brown beard and hair, he was pleasant to look at, though not
particularly handsome.

"What other mountains have you been on, Craig?"

"Just Rainier. It was a four-day clinic that was designed to
prepare climbers for Denali."

"Four days to get ready for Denali? You're kidding."

"Nope. I know. I don't think it's anywhere near enough,
either. How about you . . . what mountains have you been on?"

I briefly took him through the shopping list of summits.

"Wow. I know who I'm going to be leaning on."

I smiled. I was beginning to feel very comfortable around

Craig and extremely happy he was going to be my tentmate. I sensed that he had great compassion and strength and that any macho tendencies were carefully controlled or nonexistent. Unlike Vern who suddenly blustered into the room.

Vern was an unavoidable forty-year-old, five-foot-eight man with a bulbous nose, wire-rimmed spectacles, and a little potbelly. If not for his height, he might have easily passed for one of the Seven Dwarfs. Although I had just met him, I already had the impression that Vern had been everywhere, done everything, and knew everyone. If the conversation was about gear or him, Vern was fully engaged and spoke with obvious uninformed authority—uninformed to everyone but him. Though new to the group, he was already leaving conversations when the topic drifted to one where he was not the central figure. It didn't take long for me to figure out that if you wanted to have a conversation with the group, you did it without Vern. With Vern, the group stayed silent and just let Vern carry the day. Vern's only saving grace might be his climbing ability. He'd told everyone on the bus yesterday that he had worked his way through college climbing on the Matterhorn. I was trying very hard to like him, knowing that his bluster might be symptomatic of a nervous mouth running wild. Time would tell.

I excused myself quickly and left Craig alone with Vern (I felt bad about that for all of two seconds). Fortunately, as I was exiting, the rest of the team wandered in to share the fun.

While the rest of the team dined, I grabbed my expedition duffel and schlepped it over to the Talkeetna airport hangar. Cliff Hudson, a legendary bush pilot who had been servicing

Denali for forty-three years and had pioneered many of the glacier landings in the region, was already there, getting a Korean
team ready for their departure to the Kahiltna basecamp later
in the morning. Cliff would be flying us to Kahiltna tomorrow.

The Koreans waved at me as I entered the hangar, and I
smiled and waved back. I had seen the team the night before,
driving down Main Street brightly waving at everyone and
everything. It was funny to see them leap from their vehicle and
energetically invade the few gift shops along Main Street, emerging with armloads of whalebone carvings, scrimshaw, miniature
canoes, and other Alaskan bric-a-brac. Now, as I watched them,
they set about packing their gear with the same fervent enthusiasm. For all of their bubbling and laughter, I wondered if they
truly realized how serious an undertaking climbing Denali was.
No matter. I refocused on the task at hand, packing and checking my gear.

Robert had all of the group gear and food spread out for
inspection—tents, stoves, fuel, pots, utensils, snowshoes, snow
shovels, snow saws, radio, signal flares, wands (trail markers for
low visibility), ropes, climbing hardware, sleds, repair kit, medical kit, and an assortment of candy, oatmeal, peanut butter, hot
cocoa, pita bread, and packaged freeze-dried meals that included
lots of fat and salt—an unimaginably unhealthy diet for anyone
other than a mountaineer. We would need every ounce of fat to
help our bodies stay warm in subzero temperatures, and added
salt would assist in retaining water.

Meticulously I spread out my gear, too: crampons, ice ax,
expedition boots, parka, underwear, goggles, climbing harness,

mittens, et cetera. As I was sorting, and resorting, checking, double-checking, and then triple-checking, the rest of the team strolled in and joined the organizing party.

Vern began an entertaining performance of pulling each item he would use on the trip from his duffel, announce it, fondle it, remove the price tags, and restow it. It has been said that the ability to spend money does not necessarily translate into the ability to climb—but I was hopeful here.

I glanced around the hangar and took comfort in the precise manner with which many of the others were laying out gear and repacking their loads—until my eyes rested on Paul.

On the bus ride up, he had sat down beside me for a brief moment, long enough for me to learn that he was a pilot whose entire world seemed to revolve around planes. He was a thin, five-foot-ten, unathletic-appearing thirty-five-year-old with distinctive Greek features and jet-black hair.

I had assumed pilots were extremely organized since they have to perform a litany of tasks in sequential order before each flight, during each flight, and before each landing. Yet here was Paul, surrounded by a pile of stuff that resembled closet clutter more than essential gear for preserving life and limb. I was getting nervous just watching him pick up an item, gaze at it blankly, put it back in the pile, and then pick it up again.

"Paul? You okay over there?" I am sure that my voice did not reflect the tone of someone calmly offering assistance.

"Ahh, yeah, I guess."

"Want some help?" I felt sorry for him and prayed that his jitters would stay down here in the hangar and not follow him up onto the mountain.

"Well, sure. Yeah, that'd be great. I just borrowed this stuff from friends and I've been too busy to really go through it all—actually, this is the first time I've looked at most of this crap."

It was all I could do to keep my eyes from rolling back into my head. I also resisted the almost uncontrollable urge to lecture him firmly and point out the obvious: "Our lives and our success as well as your life depend very much on you being able to take care of yourself up there. Did it ever occur to you that checking out your gear might have been a good idea before arriving here?" Instead, I smiled through tightened lips.

"Okay, Paul. Let's get it done."

With the two of us working together, we were able to be sure all of his gear worked and get it repacked fairly swiftly.

Once all the gear was stowed and ready for tomorrow's departure, we filtered back to town. Cliff, in a wonderful gesture, offered me a ride to the motel in a pickup that had more dents than a golf ball. I clambered in and was welcomed by his miniature poodle who promptly decided that, since I was now occupying its seat, it would occupy my lap.

We drove past Sparky's Hamburgers, a small blue building with a single Order and Pick Up window and outdoor seating. While eating outside in the balmy 30-degree temperatures didn't seem ideal, I'd pretty much sampled the other available Talkeetna cuisine and was looking for variety. Since it had been closed the night before, I asked Cliff how the food was and if it would be open tonight. Indeed it would be, he said, adding that he and his wife were the owners. He went on to say that they had named the restaurant after their previous dog who met his demise as an appetizer for a hungry German shepherd. I pondered the ironically bizarre association of an establishment that specializes in serving ground meat being named after a pet poodle that had been eaten. A curious epitaph indeed. Hamburgers for dinner it would be, if for no other reason than out of respect.

After dinner, we went to the movies. We had a mandatory film-showing to attend at the Denali Park Service Ranger Station, a log building located just off Main Street designed in early modern two-car garage motif. The goal of the film, according to the presiding ranger, was to instruct all climbing teams regarding safety and environmental ethics before they headed out. We slouched down on folding chairs and prepared ourselves for the "entertainment." Nervous chatter and quips about the lack of popcorn and Goobers at this theater echoed around the room until we were shushed and the lights dimmed.

The host's voice droned on and on in a stupefying government-trained monotone. We were informed that Denali was 20,320 feet high and the tallest mountain on the North American continent, as if we didn't already know that. We were informed of other "essential facts" that they assumed we didn't know—the weather was unpredictable, very violent, and often extremely cold. . . . "No shit? So I should leave the beach chair at home?" piped up one of our team's many faceless comedians. We all snickered.

"No warning. No time. Denali is treacherous and you can't trust her no matter how good she looks," the voice droned on and on and on, and we kept quipping and snickering until death arrived on the screen.

The voice became an inconsequential murmur, a background

humming behind a mind-bending series of scenes filled with grisly shots of frostbitten toes, fingers, feet. The visuals were horrific. The voice began reading journal excerpts as I struggled to tune back in:

"As we made our way slowly down, we were surprised to see figures ahead. We could make out two climbers sitting in the snow, with equipment strewn all around them. . . . They were two lads of about twenty. One was wearing a black silk glove that had ripped apart to reveal yellow fingers, frozen solid; the other was just sitting stupefied in the snow, his head bowed over his own useless, frozen hands. Yellow Fingers was quite chirpy; joking at the coincidence of our meeting at the summit like this. Dougal asked why his hands were exposed, and received a confident, flip reply. We told him that he had frostbite, and that he would probably lose his fingers, and maybe his entire hand. 'What do you mean, frostbite?' asked Yellow Fingers. We patiently explained, got his gloves and other clothes out of his sac, and did what we could to make them both warmer. . . . We heard later that the two lads had to face extensive amputation of fingers, toes, hands, and feet, despite the finest treatment available at Anchorage Hospital." (Doug Scott)

More images of frozen body parts, blackened, blistered, yellow, green. And the voice droned on:

"Today we descended from our camp on the West Rib at 16,000 feet to 11,200 feet on the West Buttress in what was one of the most terrifying days I have ever spent in the mountains. By the time we arrived at camp below Windy Corner (12,500 feet), the gusts were in excess of one hundred miles per hour and gusting once every twenty seconds. The effort and likelihood of getting a wall up was equivalent to the risk and effort of getting to a lower elevation, so we continued to descend. The winds continued to increase as we continued down. One of the gusts knocked all nine of us to the snow. I got up quickly during a brief lull and completely to my surprise I was swept into the air and flew until my rope came tight.

That gust must have been in excess of 150 miles per hour. I don't ever recall a feeling of such helplessness in the mountains. Had it not been for the fact that most of the rest of the team were still trying to get up, it's quite possible we all could have been swept off the mountain and down onto the Peter's Glacier several thousand feet below." (Michael Covington)

The camera panned across lines of twisted flesh and broken bones that had once been living, breathing climbers like ourselves, now victims of avalanches, sudden wind gusts, crevasses, violent weather. Perhaps they, too, had watched a similar film, never imagining they would end up as its shock-value star attraction. The voice droned on about how essential it is to get down and to get down safely—the film's repetitive theme.

My eyes drifted around the room. No one was laughing. The joke was on us. Eyes were squinted in shock and amazement, lips pursed, foreheads creased. Craig caught my eye and offered a tense smile in return. All I could do was shake my head in disbelief. Robert, catching this exchange of emotion, winked at both of us. I felt better. A wink would not be enough for some of the others, however.

Vern grabbed Robert's arm as he was ducking out of the film room. "Christ, Robert! What are the chances of us ending up like, like . . . well, shit, like some of those others in that film?"

Robert smiled gently. In a calm and level voice he began to reassure the group while answering Vern's sudden panic.

"Nobody can predict Denali, any more than you can predict what is going to happen in your life tomorrow. Yes, the mountain has a reputation, and yes, people have died because of that reputation. Anything can happen on any mountain. Anything can happen anywhere. What you have to trust is that we are ready to meet anything and get through it, alive and in one piece. We're as tight as a drum and everything's buttoned down."

Robert looked around at all of the faces and began to laugh. "Hey, I'm your best evidence—still here and still with all my fingers and toes after seven trips on this mountain. Try not to allow the film to get to you, okay?"

We all nodded and filed out into the Alaskan night. Although Robert's pep talk had lifted our spirits and reassured troubled hearts, the mood was colder than the air swirling around the mountain of our dreams. I dismissed the chill as pre-climb jitters, not unusual in any circumstance. We quietly wished each other good night before retreating to our rooms and the solitude of our inner thoughts—alone we would have to wrestle with the demons conjured up by the film.

Although I knew I needed sleep, my mind wouldn't allow it. Frozen and broken bodies kept flash-framing through my brain. I squeezed my eyes to shut out the grisly pictures, to stop them from interrupting my thoughts and my sleep. I flopped over in bed for the hundredth time and resolved to sleep. In short order, the darkness of the room enveloped my soul.

SUNDAY. MAY 3
Day one on the mountain

Steam swirled around me as I luxuriated in the last shower I would be taking for at least twenty-one days. Despite the relaxing pulse of hot water, my mind was ablaze with energy. I ran through a mental checklist of things to do: fill water bottles, double-check gear, pack up personal goods I'd be leaving behind, call Bob and remind him to water house plants. I dressed quickly, so focused I hardly felt the dent in the wall my head must have left when I bent over to secure my boots—six-foot wide rooms are not intended for six-foot-tall people!

I trundled into breakfast, early again, and joined the only other member of the team seated, Jack. Jack and Vern had so far appeared inseparable—virtual clones. They even dressed alike and had shopped together for this trip. Same color Gore-Tex suits, each sporting the same brand-new creases. Scary! This was the first time I'd managed to catch Jack alone. Over a quick meal of eggs and bacon, and after some coaxing, I learned that Jack was forty-one and a computer consultant of some kind from California. We shared a common bond—leaving spouses at home who, while not overly happy about our chosen endeavors, tried very hard to be supportive of them and actually encourage us. I also learned that Jack didn't like to talk much, a perfect complement to his friend Vern who was like a television you couldn't turn off. I tired of playing conversational crowbar and elected to enjoy the silence.

Stomach full, I grabbed my remaining gear and headed over to the hangars. Four tiny single-engine, four-person Cessna 185s, equipped with snow skids, waited to ferry us the 250 miles to Kahiltna Basecamp. Our gear was already stowed, crammed and jammed into every available space within the narrow confines of each fuselage. Once we were packed into the cockpit, Cliff and the other three pilots gunned the engines and we rolled out onto the tarmac, and then, with a shove of the throttle, we were racing down the runway and soon airborne.

Timberline slipped from view shortly after we departed, immersing us in a world of ice and snow. I felt like an insect, winging its way over an unfathomable sweep of endless glaciers and broken chunks of blue ice. The enormity of Alaska and the mountain we were about to climb was sinking in. With a simple flick of its finger of fate, Denali could squash me as easily as I crushed an irritating mosquito. Up and up we climbed, rising with the mountain so that its features were never far from reach. As our 40-minute flight drew to a close, we approached what was, perhaps, the most thrilling part of any flight into the basecamp: One Shot Pass, a jagged slot so narrow that a plane's wings cleared the rock walls on either side by mere feet. Conditions had to be good. Any turbulence and One Shot was a no-go, leaving basecamp cut off from the outside world. We slipped through without a problem and touched down onto the basecamp airstrip—a swath of snow stomped smooth with snowshoes and defined by a row of black garbage bags.

As I stepped out onto the snow, I was impressed by the surreal beauty of the glacial setting. The true summit of Denali towered in the distance, filling the sky. Rock walls, soaring 3,000 to 5,000 feet above us, adorned with ice and snow that clung to their faces, encircled us on three sides. This amphitheater of rock and ice opened onto the Kahiltna Glacier, an amazing forty-mile carpet of creeping ice and snow filled with concealed crevasses, many of them large enough to swallow a tour bus and still be hungry for more.

As I stood there in awe, I contemplated what Doug Geeting, a bush pilot, had once said of Denali: "The mountain is . . . a living and breathing thing. It's been known to eat people. It gobbles them up. It's windy. It's noisy. It's just very alive."

I had no problem with the mountain being alive. I just prayed that it had lost its appetite. Working feverishly, we unloaded what seemed to be an endless amount of gear: packs, duffels, snowshoes, crampons, ice axes, ski poles, cooking stoves, gallons of fuel, ropes, rescue gear, tents, and our twenty-one-day supply of food. If things went as planned, we would be back here and off the mountain in seventeen days, but we had packed extra food just in case. After helping the pilots to spin their planes around into the wind, we ducked as they gunned their engines, sending spindrift flying. The force of the prop blast has been known to scatter the unsuspecting team's gear in all directions. Fortunately, our gear was well secured and the only thing we suffered was a dusting of snow. As the planes faded to tiny specks against the backdrop of the mountain's walls, and silence lowered down onto the scene like a heavy curtain, I finally began to get the sense that our expedition to the summit had truly begun.

The magnificence and very presence of Denali exceeded my expectations, and the power of the place easily justified the mountain's stature as a global sacred site. Standing amid this stunning drama confirmed the long-held beliefs of many cultures that such places were reserved only for gods. Mountains bear a religious connotation throughout the world. In Tibet, locals construct rock shrines and hang prayer flags on peaks and passes in recognition of these sacred sites. A similar religious attitude surrounded Aconcagua in Argentina where religious shrines cluttered the trailhead, ensuring alpinists one final opportunity to make monetary offerings on behalf of their safety. Vendors sold rosaries to be worn around the necks of the faithful as they embarked on their ascents, prompting me to wonder if they knew something we didn't. Commerce and religion have an uncanny way of intersecting along the paths to salvation— something televangelists have realized all too clearly.

On Denali, instead of icons ensuring our spiritual well-being, our necks bore two objects of more immediate corporeal significance. A butane lighter tied to a cord would provide our sole source of precious fire, while a knife hung readily accessible should we ever need to free ourselves rapidly from a climbing rope–turned–death trap. Joe Simpson recounts in his book, *Touching the Void,* that having just reached the summit of a 21,000-foot peak in the Andes, he plunged off the vertical face of an ice ledge, shattering his leg. In the hours that followed, darkness fell and a blizzard engulfed both him and his partner, Simon Yates, as Yates struggled to lower Simpson to safety. Simpson fell one more time, and was left dangling out of sight and earshot of his friend Yates. Finally, Yates was agonizingly forced to cut the rope, moments before he would have been pulled to his own death. No knife and both Yates and Simpson might have died. As it turned out, both miraculously lived. I prayed the knife around my neck would stay unopened.

The cold impressed me immediately. I could remove my gloves for only a few seconds before my skin began to take on the mottled hue of flesh beginning to freeze. I made a mental note to be very careful about what I exposed to the elements and for how long. I had every intention of getting home with the same number of working body parts as when I left.

Building snow platforms, setting up tents on them, and then constructing ice-block walls to shield the tents from potentially destructive blasts of fast-moving arctic storms, was the first task. Everyone pitched in willingly, which was a good sign.

Franklin, a six-foot-three powerhouse with curly brown hair flecked with gray, attacked building our tent city with the most enthusiasm. An assistant city manager from Arizona, he reveled in thrusting the saw into the ground and then laboring to produce perfectly shaped blocks of ice that we would then engineer into place, forming impervious walls. I was fascinated by this bundle of energy.

"Planning on building a deck and sauna to go with the city you're erecting, Franklin?"

He smiled broadly. "If you're gonna do something, you may as well do it right, don't ya think, Ruth Anne?"

"Absolutely, Franklin, absolutely. You're quite adept at cutting those blocks. This can't be your first big mountain, then."

His smile softened somewhat, but still remained. "I tried for the summit last year. . . . Didn't make it, though. . . . Got pulmonary edema and had to go down. . . . Shame, really." He stopped cutting blocks for a second and looked toward the summit. "I promised both of my daughters that I'd make it this time, and I will, you know."

"I don't doubt that for a minute." I hardly knew this man, and yet I already admired him.

"Pulmonary edema? Oh man, that's kind of a drag." The voice belonged to Randy, a six-foot-two, thirty-six-year-old, Denver-based restaurateur with a slim, athletic build and a razzle-dazzle, "groovy, what's happenin'" kind of attitude. Just watching him, I surmised that he was wiry, agile, buoyant, and tireless, in a nervous sort of way. Randy also had an outstanding sense of humor and was the main instigator behind the giggling and snickering during the previous night's infamous film—that is until the pictures punched the breath out of all our laughter.

Franklin just laughed. "Yeah, I guess it was 'kind of a drag' at that."

Yes, pulmonary edema is a drag. It can kill, and the fact that Franklin was back after a bout with it was a testament to his mental fortitude. Pulmonary edema strikes without warning. There is no way of anticipating who will or will not develop this or any other form of altitude sickness and physical fitness is absolutely no assurance of safety. Franklin must have known that just because he had gotten sick before did not mean he would get sick again. On the other hand, it is possible he or any of us could come down with pulmonary edema and have to suffer an evacuation—weather permitting.

Once the last tent was up, a scramble of gear-tossing and male bonding left Craig standing alone with me, the lone female. It seemed no other man wanted to share Craig's fate, which he accepted graciously. Fate has its rewards, however, and we were both smugly pleased when we realized that our housing situation was the best of them all. While the others would be crammed three deep in their tents, Craig and I would wallow luxuriously in a few precious inches of space. I also knew that having one fewer body in the tent to climb over, around, or under, would serve as a valuable energy conserver.

A variety of chores filled the afternoon hours. Some of us taped flags onto wands, the thin bamboo poles used to mark the route and keep us out of harm's way around camp— mountaineers have fallen to their deaths in crevasses just a few feet from their tents simply because they hadn't taken the time to mark a safe boundary. Others sorted gear, filled fuel tanks, divided and repackaged food, and rigged the sleds to be dragged up the glacier the following day.

Robert's sister, who lived in Alaska, had come to Talkeetna earlier that morning to see him off, and she showered him with homemade gifts. A small pillow decorated with dinosaurs was carefully stowed in his pack and Robert informed us he had every intention of taking "Dino and friends" all the way to the summit. One of the other gifts, a blueberry pie, managed to survive only several hours before triggering a sharklike feeding frenzy among the ten of us.

That night, as Craig and I lay warm in our sleeping bags, we listened to snippets of conversation that floated with the mountain air into our tent. Paul was telling his two tentmates, Franklin and John—a six-foot-three, thirty-nine-year-old, married New York attorney with a runner's build and a successful summit of Aconcagua under his belt—about a recent climb up Rainier. Seems Paul found himself in a rather curious predicament: that of having to decide how to keep his pants up—(they were beginning to slip down toward his ankles) without letting go of either the rope (his lifeline) or his ice ax. Paul appeared rather proud of the fact that he managed to summit while clinging to his pants, tripping and stumbling over the loose fabric every step of the way.

"Should Paul have trouble with his pants on this trip, I'll be all too happy to help him secure them—around his neck," Craig muttered quietly.

"Not if I get to help him first," I whispered back.

We exchanged glances and broke into laughter.

MONDAY, MAY 4
Day two on the mountain

Let the slogging begin. After a quick breakfast and taking the time to stow gear we would not need in a carefully prepared snow cave, we shouldered sixty-pound packs and strapped ourselves into our sled harnesses. The additional fifty pounds of gear slipping along behind me felt rather like an anchor. Our goal was Camp II, five miles away and only 1,000 feet higher at 8,000 feet.

It was one boot in front of the other. The weight tugging at my waist and on my shoulders felt new and strangely unnatural. Snow crunched and squeaked loudly under each footfall. My breath sounded heavy. In fact, everything about me felt heavy. We worked our way up the Kahiltna Glacier, through a wonderland of monolithic ice formations and scenery carved by the glacial activity surrounding us. Several ravens, swooping and cawing overhead, were the only other living things that dared to move in this white-and-blue world, adding a somewhat Hitchcock-esque mood to the trek.

Vern, apparently was feeling heavy, too, despite the nearly constant stream-of-consciousness about gear and climbing suggestions that spouted from his mouth. In fact, he informed us he was feeling sick during our first rest break.

"Oh geez . . . oh shiiiit . . . oh god, I don't feel good. I'm real beat and light-headed."

"Vern, if you would spend less time talking and more time walking, we might actually get somewhere, like camp, by the end of the day!" Craig, who was just ahead of Vern on the rope, was getting a bit irritated at having to drag what he had privately referred to me as "a babbling deadweight" up the mountain.

Robert, taking stock of the situation, determined that Vern was suffering from lack of fluid intake and made him begin taking sips from his bottle.

"A bit different than the Matterhorn, isn't it, Vern?" chided Randy.

"He's not suffering from altitude or fatigue," chimed in Paul. "Vern's suffering from speech deprivation brought on by an inability to breathe heavily and speak at the same time."

Despite all the ribbing he was getting, Vern managed to maintain his relentlessly irritating cheerfulness. "Climbing the Matterhorn at Disneyland for a summer wasn't anything like this, that's for sure!"

"DISNEYLAND!" we all echoed together.

I remembered that Vern had said he climbed the Matterhorn in college for work and thought how easily I had assumed the word "work" translated into "guide," which implied climbing experience.

"I was one of the climbers that went up the Matterhorn several times a day for the visitors to see," Vern said proudly.

Perfect. So much for his one saving grace.

We continued up the mountain, and Vern continued babbling. By mid-afternoon, we reached Camp II, located just above the northwest buttress of Mount Francis in a large, level area below Ski Hill. It had taken us all of five hours. I could see the Korean team's camp in the distance. With their brightly colored team uniforms, they appeared as bits of confetti scattered on a field of white.

Franklin, Craig, Randy, John, Paul, Jack, and I all set about quickly digging tent platforms, building the ice-block walls and getting the tents pitched. Vern, sick with altitude, rested nearby. No sooner were the tents up than we all scurried for shelter.

The temperature was holding steady at near zero—cold enough to freeze the tail off a polar bear. After a quick meal, I dove into the warm confines of my sleeping bag, too.

"Only five miles today, and still the big talkers were suckin' wind," chuckled Craig as I made myself comfortable. "Yesterday, Vern couldn't stop telling everyone how good he was and how much his gear cost and where it came from and who made it, and look at him today. I practically had to carry his ass up to camp. And Paul. Didn't he say he had been training with a 110-pound pack or something like that?"

"I believe he did say something about 110 pounds," I whispered, not wanting the other tents to hear our conversation.

"Well, if he did, he sure managed to get out of shape fast, 'cause sixty pounds was killing him today. Even Vern's pal Jack was moaning about the weight."

"They'll learn or they won't make it," I assured Craig, although I wasn't all that sure they would learn, either. All of them needed to relax and stop fighting the altitude—work with it by focusing and breathing. Mountaineering is about conserving energy. I had figured out long ago that successful mountaineers learn to harness the mountain's energy, not fight it. I call it the "inner game of climbing." Focus on the objective, not the distance or the obstacles. Once you get there, you know it. It becomes an almost unconscious effort . . . a little magical.

"At least Paul's pants stayed up," I giggled, trying to lighten the mood.

Craig laughed. "We've still got another sixteen days for those babies to come down."

{3} THE DRESS REHEARSAL

Day three on the mountain

M y thermometer read 0 degrees Fahrenheit. Inside the tent, a thick layer of frost blanketed everything. Even the water bottles, which I had forgotten to place inside my sleeping bag, had frozen.

"Morning, Craig, and welcome to another balmy day."

He sat up, showering me with a dusting of ice particles that broke loose from his sleeping bag.

"Oh man, I'm tired.... What's it like outside?" Craig flopped back down.

I scooted forward, taking great delight in returning the frost-dusting favor and leaving Craig spluttering. As I poked my head out the door of our tent, the brilliance of the morning blinded me.

"Deep blue and bright white are the colors of the day!" I exclaimed. "It is simply incredible out here."

Only a light breeze stirred. Robert and Win were up and heating water for breakfast.

"Since you're already sitting up, Ruth Anne, why don't you go ahead and get dressed first."

On the surface, Craig's gesture appeared most chivalrous but in a wickedly cold tent, I suspected that he was just as eager to spend a few extra minutes snuggled in his warm bag. I'd have to remember to time my morning better tomorrow and make him sit up first.

In the confines of a tent, getting dressed requires a coordinated dance whose movements are limited by the amount of available space. Depending on who was getting dressed, the other would roll over on his side to provide as much working room as possible. Since sleeping in long underwear and often expedition fleece and a down vest was requisite, the first item of the day was my expedition parka. The next order of business was to locate my glove liners and mittens. I slipped on the liners and placed my mittens nearby. I pulled off my down booties, which I slept in, and replaced them with socks I had been keeping warm in my sleeping bag. Next, being very careful not to knock too much frost loose into either my sleeping bag or onto Craig, I unfurled my expedition Gore-Tex bibs—a bit like working with cardboard since they would freeze each night from the moisture that accumulated both inside and outside the fabric layers. Wriggling like a caterpillar trying to crawl out of a cocoon (in this case, I was trying to get back in), I wormed my way into the stiff fabric. By this point, I was breathing like a bull about to charge the matador.

"Hey, Ruth Anne, could you hold it down? I'm trying to get a few extra minutes of sleep here," Craig quipped.

"You just wait. Your turn's coming and then I'll be the one laughing."

Taking a deep breath to slow my breathing, I slid my feet into my frozen boot-liners. Boot-liners do keep your feet warm when you are moving, but first thing in the morning, this little task offers all the pleasure of sliding your feet into a bowlful of frozen Jell-O and leaving them there. I wanted to get moving and fast. I laced up the liners, shoved my feet into the plastic boots, secured them, tugged on my mittens, zipped up my parka, and dove out the door into the brilliant light.

Before heading off to the latrine, I turned and poked my head back in the door.

"Your turn . . . welcome to my misery!"

As I headed off, I could hear Craig yelping with the cold, as much for show, I'm sure.

We each took our turn with various camp chores—latrine-digging was one. I had found out the night before that volunteering for this duty was not without its hazards. The first duty of the latrine team was to determine a safe spot to place the latrine—preferably nowhere near a crevasse or in the path of an avalanche. Once a safe spot no more than twenty-five yards from camp had been located, the latrine team marked the route with wands so that in the event of a whiteout, you could answer Mother Nature's call without fear of straying from camp. Next, using a saw, ice blocks were cut from the glacier and used to start a "privacy wall" that surrounds the latrine on three sides. When completed, the wall stands waist-high, allowing a 360-degree view of the area when conducting negotiations, while making it obvious to those on the sidelines that the latrine was occupied. Once the ice blocks were cut, a three-foot-deep hole was dug into the snow and lined with a garbage bag that was secured to two more ice blocks being used to make a suitable throne. Digging this hole always filled the latrine construction crew with a certain amount of dread—it wouldn't be the first time a latrine-goer had actually dug themselves right through a snow bridge and into the gaping mouth of a crevasse. The finishing touch was applied by hanging a roll of toilet paper wrapped in a baggie on an ice ax.

Robert once dryly remarked that if a snow bridge ever gave way while one of us was perched on the latrine, we could use the ice ax to arrest our fall. While the words offered slight comfort, I was never too sure just how one performed a self-arrest with pants around the ankles. Yep, digging a latrine was a hazardous duty indeed.

Sitting at breakfast, our senses were jolted into full alert by a violent explosion. The snow under our feet shook and the air reverberated.

"My God!" John practically dropped a cup of cocoa in his lap in his haste to stand up.

Robert and Win were fully focused, showing no emotion.

All our eyes fixed on a 16,000-foot peak about a mile away from camp. A huge slab, almost 5,000 feet worth, of snow and ice had just sheared off its face, exposing the bedrock underneath. For five minutes, no one spoke as we watched a cloud of snow generated from the impact billow up almost 3,000 feet into the air—a plume large enough to swallow Squaw Valley in California, or Colorado's Ajax Mountain in Aspen. I had read about wind blasts from avalanches tearing into camps and shredding everything that lay in their path. I was very glad we were far enough away to appreciate the magnitude of the event without actually becoming part of it.

"Quite impressive, isn't it?" Robert mused aloud as he and Win went back to prepping for the day.

"Wow, like that was one hell of a show, you know, man? I mean, it toasted everything in its path." Leave it to Randy to put the perfect capper on the moment.

With the "show" over and breakfast stowed in our stomachs, it was time to shoulder our loads and get back to the task at hand—shuttling gear, otherwise known as "doing a carry," up the mountain. Camp III would be at 9,500 feet and our goal was to shuttle half of our gear up to the camp, cache it in the snow, and then return to Camp II by evening to eat dinner and sleep. Although this appears to be a waste of effort to many, there is a method to the madness. Often, the insidious effects of altitude occur during sleep cycles when breathing patterns are irregular. By trying to bite off the entire 1,500-foot elevation gain in one trip, we would be upping the effort-meter and then sleeping higher, too, doubling the opportunity for one or more of us to get altitude sickness. By doing carries to a high point, and then sleeping at a low point, we effectively extended our acclimatization period, even though this technique meant we would be climbing the mountain twice.

Up we went, one step at a time, with Robert and Win on full alert for avalanches and crevasses. As we crossed crevasse fields, a rope always linked us together. Crevasses come in all shapes and sizes, and I had been lowered into them during practice rescues. Beautiful yet deadly, their vertical walls of blue ice disappear menacingly into darkness. Many of the ones we passed by, gaping hungrily at the sky, yielded no sound or hint as to their depth when we tossed a rock or two in them. Other times, crevasses appeared with little or no warning. Subtle undulations, little more than mere shadows against a white sheet of snow suggested a veiled trap that we should step over or around, but never on.

Robert was in front of me on the rope as we moved across an unbroken and open field of snow when he fell through up to his waist. It happened so suddenly that I barely had time to stop and sink my ice ax into the snow to arrest his fall. Those behind me readied themselves for the impending shock of a fall that never came. Robert wriggled his way carefully out of the hole, more annoyed than anything.

"I don't usually get surprised like that," he muttered to no one in particular. Then louder for all to hear, "Watch this hole as you come across."

It was frightening stepping across a black hole knowing that where you were placing your feet was simply a sliver of snow crust that could give way at any moment. I felt like I was walking on egg shells.

"Think light thoughts," I yelled to Craig.

"Don't worry, I'm thinking so light I might just float away," Craig fired back.

"Hey, Vern, just hold your breath and harness some of that hot air for flotation," quipped Randy.

Nervous laughter washed over the team. Vern muttered some unintelligible comment into his beard.

They say that when a crevasse is black, the depth exceeds 100 feet. All those we saw this day were black. Some appeared deceptively benign as mere slits on the surface, while on closer inspection I could see that they actually opened into vast dome-shaped caverns below. Others spanned many feet, gradually becoming tighter as they reached greater depths. Lodged in such a "squeezer," a victim's breathing would seal his fate as with each breath he will sink deeper and deeper until the crevasse squeezes so tightly he is unable to breathe again.

In 1981, Jim Wickwire (who was, coincidentally, climbing Denali with world-renowned mountaineer John Roskelley on the same route and at the same time as we were) and his partner, twenty-five-year-old Rainier guide Chris Kerrebrock, were attempting a new route on the seldom-climbed Wickersham Wall of Denali. After crossing a very nasty ice field successfully, Wickwire and Kerrebrock broke through on what appeared to be a smooth and clean slope. Wickwire fell on top of Kerrebrock, who was now wedged like a cork, head down. Despite having broken his left shoulder, Wickwire managed to put on his crampons and unfasten his ice hammer so that he could work his way out of the eighteen-inch-wide crevasse. Once on the surface, he set up a haul system with his jumars and a snow picket and tried to move Kerrebrock. He couldn't. According to Wickwire, nothing he tried would work to remove Kerrebrock. Wickwire lay on the edge of the crevasse, comforting his companion until he took his last breath, nine hours after having fallen in. Denali is a hungry mountain.

"Oh shit!"

Paul, just behind me on the rope, screamed as he mimicked Robert's waist-deep plunge just minutes before.

Unlike Robert, Paul panicked, flailing about while trying to extricate himself.

"Stay calm!" Win admonished, but his advice fell on deaf ears.

Somehow, Paul managed to pull himself out of the hole without bringing the entire snow bridge crashing down around him and us. "WOW . . . did you see that? Just tried to swallow me whole. Oh my gosh!" His voice came in pants and wheezes.

We called back a warning to the other team behind us to watch for the hidden snow bridge and then moved on and up. Despite all the effort we were expending and the knot-up-your-gut fear of falling into a crevasse we were all experiencing, Vern was still blathering on. It was truly incredible how many words he could manage to fit in between gasps for air. If only he could shut up, he might be able to harness the energy he was wasting. But, that would be asking for too much. Vern's mouth, like the Energizer Bunny, just kept going and going and going.

As we were nearing the crest of Ski Hill, a not-very-steep incline, I noticed another group, a team of five, marching toward us. They were unloaded, so they must have just completed their carry to Camp III. We were so close to them it appeared as if we were sharing the same lane of traffic and one of us would have to move to allow the other by. Just as I was preparing myself to offer a greeting it happened.

The leader must have hooked a crampon because with no warning, the entire team was tumbling, rolling, twisting in the rope. They were still tied together yet each climber was moving in independent, frantic, out-of-control motions—flailing arms and legs, feet first and then head first and then broadside. Their rate of acceleration was impressive, especially on so gradual a slope. No one on their team appeared to be attempting a self-arrest, leaving them caught in an unchecked free fall. It happened so fast that all we could do was brace ourselves for the inevitable impact as they swept into us like a bowling ball crashes into a row of arranged pins. Miraculously, they flew by us, brushing so close I could feel the wind generated by their passing on my face. My biggest worry was that, with them being so close, an arm might reach out to grab us or a loose ice ax might snag one of our legs as it bounced by. What I remember most, though, was the silence of their passing. No screams or cries of panic. Just the dull thud of bodies tumbling on ice accompanied by the muffled clanking of metal and the occasional "oomph" and groan.

We watched their slide into oblivion slow as they swept out onto level snow. I became conscious of my fingers clenched so tightly around my ice ax that the circulation had been cut off. I began breathing as each of their team rose unsteadily, dusted themselves off and then waved at us that all was okay. Fortunately, it appeared that all they had suffered were the odd bruises and perhaps blows to the ego that come with surviving such a fall.

Without a word, we turned and began the final push to Camp III. Even Vern was silent.

WEDNESDAY, MAY 6
Day four on the mountain

The distant summit of Denali seemed to attract every cloud in the sky. Last night, a cap of lenticular clouds was forming over the upper half of the mountain. By morning, the peak was completely engulfed, indicating deadly shear winds aloft and signaling the mountain's most violent conditions. I stared at the summit for a while, curious that it was so calm here, yet just miles away, so turbulent. I wondered if any poor souls were experiencing the misfortune of being on or near the summit during the height of this weather change—I hoped not, for their sake.

We listened to the forecasts received from Fairbanks on our tiny radio each day, but found they had little or no bearing on our situation. The massive hulk of Denali either generated its own weather or compounded existing systems, turning them into a redirected force to be reckoned with.

After breaking camp, we began the trek up to Camp III and our food-and-gear cache left from the carry we did yesterday. The effort was tortuous as my boots broke through wind-crusted snow, throwing me repeatedly forward. The weight of my pack threatened to slam me facefirst into the snow each time I stumbled. How easy Kilimanjaro now seemed, where the luxury of porters had been enjoyed.

Just before heading up Ski Hill, where our group of human bowling pins had almost been struck out by the tumble of another team, we took an extended break.

There, reclining on the snow, I savored a candy bar and sipped from my bottle of ice-cold water. The rest was heavenly. All around me, the other members of the team had kicked back. Craig, sitting near me, turned to answer a question, pivoting his weight onto his left knee, and the snow gave way.

"Oh, sweet Jesus!" Craig's face had gone white. There was nothing under his knee except a yawning, black hole. Fortunately, he hadn't committed his weight to that knee, and remained balanced precariously, sitting on his heels while leaning as hard on his right knee as he dared. None of us was prepared to arrest his fall. Worse, the knowledge that we were all probably sitting on a large, brittle flake of snow just waiting to give way swept through my stomach and flooded my nerves. I tried to swallow, but couldn't.

"Don't move—not one inch," said Robert. "When I tell you, slowly work your way toward me. Stay calm and make sure your movements are very slow, gentle, and controlled. Can you do that?" Robert must have ice water running through his veins.

Craig nodded. We were all painfully aware that he would get only one chance to move. If Robert directed him to go the wrong way, the rest of the flake could collapse and he would pitch headfirst into the hole, dragging those of us attached to his rope with him.

He began to edge toward Robert, never taking his eyes off him for one second. Bits of snow peeled away from the edge of the black hole as the flake flexed ever so slightly under Craig's weight.

"Come on Craig, easy does it."

Craig inched his way toward Robert, taking what seemed to me an eternity to cover merely six feet. Every slight shift of weight made the snow creak.

Once Craig was on more solid footing, Robert looked around at each of us. "Let's load up and move outta here, carefully."

Slowly, deliberately, we each stood, slipping arms through shoulder straps gingerly, taking extreme care not to bounce or jump. All you could hear was heavy breathing and the squeak of dry snow under boots. No one spoke. We spread out so as to distribute our weight, and moved on.

"Damn! That was close!" Craig was the first to speak.

"Uh-huh . . . too close," I whispered to no one in particular.

Denali's changing moods offer no rest and no respite. Within minutes of starting to walk, and with no warning, we were engulfed in an arctic front, sweeping down off the mountain with the force of an oncoming truck. Like everyone else on the team, I scrambled desperately to get my parka and face protection out of my pack and onto my body. I moved fast, but not fast enough. Within a minute, my face was numb.

Struggling against the sheer force of the winds, we worked our way up the final slope and to our cache. How Robert found it so easily with the snow pelting our faces is beyond me. It was the elements, in part, that had lured me to Denali. I entertained aspirations of climbing seriously in the Himalayas, and summiting Denali while surviving her ever-changing moods is considered a prerequisite—so far, I was getting everything I had asked for, and more.

"Ruth Anne?!" Robert yelled at me from a few feet away.

"Yeah?"

"Could you belay me while I secure a safe perimeter for our camp?"

With me holding on to his lifeline, Robert worked quickly, crisscrossing the camp, probing the snow looking for unseen hazards. It would be most unhealthy to pitch a tent on a snow bridge that was clinging tenuously to the gaping maw of a bottomless crevasse. While Robert placed the wands, we began to freeze.

This was a fire drill. Fifty-mile-per-hour winds are not un-usual. It could get worse, so learning to set up camp efficiently in these kinds of conditions was an essential test for our team. It didn't take long for us to break out the tools (saws and shovels) and begin building ice platforms and the ice-block walls. What we didn't foresee was the quality of the snow. It was crusty and junky, breaking apart even before we managed to complete cut-ting a block, let alone attempt to pick it up and stack it. It took two hours just to get the walls built sufficiently that they would protect our tents. By then, the rest of our gear had disappeared beneath snowdrifts.

"Oh, terrific," Craig screamed over the howl of the wind. "You seen my sled anywhere?"

"We'd better start digging to find things, or they might end up buried for good," I yelled back, even though we were stand-ing just feet apart. Keep up a conversation for long in these kind of conditions and you're liable to go hoarse.

Snow flew in all directions, mixing with the stuff that was still blowing and falling, as our team dug frantically in the snow-drifts, looking for tents and packs. Fortunately, our efforts were quickly rewarded and tents popped up without further trouble.

Our final task was to dig a hole deep enough to shelter the kitchen so that our stoves would be out of the wind. With our sleds, snowshoes, ice axes, and packs stowed safely between the tents and their ice-block walls, we paused to suck down a hot dinner. This was no sit-down affair. We ate standing up, shov-eling the food in as fast as we could move our spoons and chew our food. There would be no relaxing in the kitchen, sipping hot cocoa and swapping tales this night. No sir. It was eat and run all the way. I couldn't wait to get out of the storm and into my sleeping bag.

The onslaught of instability and the sudden realization that we were powerless before the whims of the weather gods sobered everyone. This was no nature walk, that's for sure. I shut my eyes and drifted off to the sounds of a howling wind and snow crystals hissing off the tent's nylon skin.

THURSDAY, MAY 7
Day five on the mountain

The storm was still buffeting our camp when I awoke early the next morning. A quick peek outside revealed all that I needed to know—no visibility, high winds, tons of snow. We would not be going anywhere today.

"Well?"

Craig was obviously curious, but not so curious that he wanted to look for himself.

"Socked in and pinned down, I'd say. Looks like you're stuck with me for another twenty-four hours."

"Dammit! . . . I mean about the weather, not about . . . Aww, shit. Never mind. God, I can't believe we are pinned down so early in this climb."

I smiled. Craig was not happy about the current state of affairs.

"Yeah, but there's not much we can do about it. My hope is that the mountain is getting its surly weather streak out of the way and we'll have a clear shot to the summit once this blows by."

"Oh man, I hope so, I really do. Being stuck in a tent for my entire trip is not what I had in mind for a really good time, you know, even with the best of company." Craig shot me a grin and winked.

I lay back on my sleeping pad and stared at the frost feathers coating the walls of our tent. Unless we spent the time to remove them—and soon—we could be soaking in melted frost.

"We should scrape this frost off before we begin knocking pieces of it into our sleeping bags and onto our clothes," I mused aloud.

"I suppose you're right, but they do add a nice touch to the tent's interior, don't you think?" Craig was grinning ear-to-ear. At least his mood had lightened.

We began to carefully pull down the feathers and toss as much of the frost outside the tent as possible. Suddenly, Craig began snickering, and he was armed with a camera.

Click! "You'll want to remember this moment, Ruth Anne. Shoveling the ice from inside our tent. Nice lighting, too."

Lighting? There was none. Any light that filtered through the layers of tent fabric and crystals of ice was diffused. I'd seen inside-the-tent shots before and they always make the victims appear as if they have green skin. I wasn't about to go down without sharing the misery.

"Your turn!" I grabbed the camera and Craig made a face.

Click. We both started laughing, taking great pleasure in knowing that the photos were bound to look absolutely hideous.

"Hey guys!" The tent door burst open and the hooded head that pushed its way in turned out to belong to Randy.

"Oh man, those other guys are driving me nuts! I just had to get out or I was going to kill someone for sure!"

Randy was looking a little wild-eyed, although I could understand his pain. I'd probably lose it too if I had to stay cooped up in a tent with Vern and Jack.

"Say, you two care for room service this morning? While our facilities at this fine establishment aren't much to speak of, we do pride ourselves on personalized service."

"Room service would be great—too bad you can't take care of going to the bathroom for us, too." The thought of dropping any part of my pants in this wind left me shuddering.

The tent door closed tightly as Randy zipped off to the kitchen. Breakfasts on the mountain don't amount to much in terms of flavor or variety, but they are intended to pack a fuel-punch for the day—oatmeal, hot cocoa, and granola bars were the staples. Two five-pound containers of peanut butter and jelly along with pita bread would suffice for lunches, at least that was the plan. As of yesterday's lunch, the peanut butter was frozen too hard to spread or even break off. While someone could sleep with the containers to warm them up, the thought of snuggling an ice-cold tub of peanut butter offered little appeal. The extra snacks each of us had brought would have to fill the appetite gap.

Dinners on our little adventure featured instant soup, mashed potatoes, Stove Top dressing, ramen noodles, macaroni and cheese, and the occasional tin of tuna to give flavoring or added food value to the dinner creation. Retorts (boil-in-the-bag delicacies) provided a variety of tantalizing entrées. I am of the opinion that any food group with the name "retort" deserves little respect. The mystery meat of school days past had returned to haunt me with a vengeance. When wrapped in translucent yellowed leaves, the retort resembled cabbage rolls, or so I am told, while the presence of a single pasta noodle suggested an attempt at lasagna. The same meat, smothered with gravy, qualified as steak when in one piece but when cut into cubes, we called it stew. It certainly wasn't food as I knew it, but at least it did provide fuel to heat and power my body.

Our tent door burst open again. Randy sure knew how to make an entrance. He thrust in steaming cups of cocoa followed by two bowls of oatmeal—breakfast in bed, how chic!

"Bon appetit! Now you may eat," Randy announced as he pulled himself back out of the door, disappearing into the white void that existed beyond our tent walls.

We sipped, munched, and listened to Randy clearing snow from the surrounding tents. He was doing everything in his power to keep from having to crawl back into what he referred to as "Trivial Pursuit hell."

"I can't believe it! I'll have to go back down," Randy cried. "I just checked my pack and it seems I've gone and left my snowplow behind."

Craig and I broke up laughing. At least our humor was still in good shape. One place Randy would not have to shovel was our tent. We had, quite by accident, positioned our tent so that the door did not get drifted in with snow. Everyone else, it seems, was having to dig themselves out and clear a pathway to their doors.

It wasn't until three-thirty P.M. that Craig and I ventured out. Randy had made several visits to our tent during the morning and afternoon—he was, apparently, very bored—and had insisted that I "drop by their place for a visit."

I poked my head inside. "Whaddaya think?" asked Vern eagerly.

"Well, it's the perfect picture of organization, I'd say." Vern seemed pleased at my comment. Randy just rolled his eyes.

Sleeping bags were perfectly lined up, gear stacked around the edges, and socks hanging from the interior roof to dry. Organized and tight. I couldn't get over how lucky I was at having only one tentmate and extremely fortunate I didn't have to tent with Vern.

"Hey, check this out—perfect for dining in the storm." Vern pulled a sack from his pack and held it up proudly for all to see. "Got it from one of the best outdoor stores around—a Megamid. It's a tent big enough to eat in. The store gave me a great deal since it was a factory second. Incredible, huh?"

"Yeah Vern, truly incredible," I was trying to keep the sarcasm from dripping too heavily from my lips. Not only was this man a walking Trivial Pursuit nightmare, he came to the mountain drowning in gear—only the best gear—and took too much pleasure in showing it off. If he'd pulled a solar-powered heater for the tent from his pack, I wouldn't have been surprised at all.

"So, Vern. What exactly made this tent a second and why on earth are you lugging it up the mountain?" Craig chimed in.

"Oh, it had a few fabric flaws, but nothing too serious. It'll be perfect as a kitchen tent, which is why I brought it. May as well eat dry and warm when we're working so hard each day."

Vern did have a point. Eating dry and warm would be nice, but the added energy spent lugging a few extra pounds of nylon and aluminum up the mountain canceled out any aesthetic benefit the tent may have offered, in my opinion—though I chose not to voice it to Vern.

"Fabric flaw? Fabric flaw? Yeah, that's rich, Vern. Man, it's missing the entire floor," said Randy, firing a salvo of derisive humor at Vern's ego-fortified heart.

Vern just blinked his eyes quietly, then motioned in the direction of the kitchen. "I just thought it would be nice for all of us, that's all. Without the floor it's perfect for pitching over a prepared kitchen hole in the snow, but we don't have to put it up if you guys don't want to."

"Are you kidding? This thing I gotta see," piped in Randy. "Gimme that."

We spent the next couple of hours humoring Vern by digging a new dining hole since the other one did not match the tent's dimensions.

The blizzard raged on around us while we dug. Visibility was so poor that few of us even noticed a lone climber who wandered into our camp. Icicles three inches long hung from his mustache, giving him an almost walruslike appearance. Mr. Walrus, in between gasping breaths, managed to tell us of the storm up higher. Winds were "nuking," he said, and two teams had already turned back, suffering from frostbite and exposure. According to him, no one had yet made it above 14,000 feet. As quickly and quietly as he had appeared, he vanished, slipping into the swirling white like an apparition. He wanted nothing more to do with the summit we still coveted.

Ten others, Germans, wandered into our camp soon afterward. The guide told us his team had camped just below and that they had unsuccessfully tried to go to 11,000 feet with a carry. He said he'd gotten disoriented in the near whiteout and needed a push in the right direction. I looked around at their faces, shrouded by the white haze of windblown flakes. Not one smile among the distant looks. None of them were wearing parkas, either, and they all looked borderline hypothermic. The guide, dressed in very flashy guide yellow and guide red, wore these very strange white plastic Eurosquare wraparound goggles over his eyes. Out of one pocket hung a sodden map of Denali. I wondered if this lost guide had purchased the map at the gift store in Talkeetna. One thing about flashy guide suits: They're wonderful for making sure the body gets found when the one wearing them appears to have flicked the off switch for his brain.

We sent the guide over to Robert's tent to ask directions. It was clear to me that the German team would have liked nothing better than for us to invite them into our shelters and ply them with brandy and hot cocoa. I wondered what Robert would do.

I watched the guide bend over and poke his head into Robert's tent. In a moment or two, he stood up, shrugged his shoulders, turned, and walked swiftly back to the kitchen tent and his team. He motioned and the team headed off, single file.

We wandered over to Robert's tent and he stuck his head out to talk to us.

"What was up with them?" Craig wondered aloud.

"Dumbasses. The guide has never set foot on this mountain. If they pull another stunt like this one, they'll be lucky to get off this mountain at all." Robert shook his head in disgust.

"I told 'em to follow the wands we had placed back down to their camp and I hope they follow that advice," added Robert gravely. "They're heading into a crevasse field with a guide who has no clue and that's trouble."

"How come you didn't ask them to stay here?" asked Jack. "I mean if they're in trouble and all, shouldn't we have helped them?"

"Nope. I gave them the only thing we could spare, advice. We don't have the resources to do any more than that, period."

Robert's feelings mirrored mine. Anyone on this mountain must be prepared for the worst and needs to be self-sufficient. Lack of preparation and planning by a team endangers not only that team, but anyone else who tries to help. They had chosen unwisely to go out in bad weather. They hadn't dressed properly. Their guide had never been on the mountain before. In short, their guide should have known better. Bad decisions lead to mountaineering statistics. I turned and walked back to finish building the kitchen.

Our new kitchen and dining facility was indeed grand— circular, dug five feet deep, with a sitting bench carved into the perimeter and a cooking island in the middle. In celebration, Vern and Jack volunteered to cook.

That night, after returning to the cramped quarters of our tent, Craig and I reached the conclusion that the only honorable ways for this team not to make the summit would be because of impossibly bad weather or running out of food. So there we sat, stuck at 9,500 feet, faced with the possibility of remaining tentbound until the storm blew over—in hours, or days or weeks—who knew? I broke into a fit of giggles.

"I know how we can get out of this without losing face or our sanity," I snickered.

Craig, now beginning to laugh himself, although not sure exactly why, shook his head from side to side. "No way, we're stuck here forever. There is no way out, but go on anyway."

"Look, we've decided that if we run out of food, we can't climb, right?"

"Right."

"So, if you eat like a pig for the next few days, you might just cause enough of a food shortage that we can get off this mountain with honor and not have to stay cooped up in this damn tent." Tears were now streaming down my face, I was laughing so hard.

"Thanks. Eat like a pig? What about you? Aren't you going to help out on this noble cause?" Craig was fighting to contain the laugh attack to a mere giggle.

"Hell no. I've got my figure to worry about."

That sealed it. Now we were both lost to waves of uncontrolled, hysterical laughter. We were having entirely too much of a good time for two adults stuck high on a mountain in a tiny space.

FRIDAY, MAY 8
Day six on the mountain

Plop ... ploop ... plop. I opened my eyes and watched the next drop of water land squarely between them on the bridge of my nose. Before I could roll away, another drip splashed onto my forehead. Great, being cooped up was not enough. Now I found myself subjected to a Chinese-water-torture treatment. I studied the situation and realized that moisture was collecting along the inside seam over my head, moisture caused by the heat of the sun melting the frost feathers that had built up in our tent.

Sun! I sat up, scrambled forward, and unzipped the tent door. Sure enough, the weather had broken, revealing a scattered cloud cover and glorious, wonderful, fantastic sunshine. Elated? I would have done back flips with more room. We'd been on the mountain for one week and had only climbed 1,500 feet, which was frustrating since I would climb that elevation and more from my home in the Sierra in only two hours. We were moving slower than the glaciers we were climbing. At this rate, the next Ice Age would set in before we summited.

"Hot dog! We'll be climbing today for sure," I practically screamed.

"Thank God. I am sooo tired of just hangin' around!" said Craig.

"I hear that. If I intended to spend a vacation lying around, I would have booked a trip to a tropical beach and not this massive ice cube." I was already pulling on my clothes, fumbling for my boots and planning my escape.

While we were readying our sleds for the carry to 11,500 feet, Robert strode over.

"Craig, since we're carrying half loads, I was wondering if you'd mind hauling an extra package along for us to crevasse on the way." Robert had a wry smile as he made the request.

The package Robert had in mind was the latrine's garbage

bag, now very full. Denali Park rules stipulate that teams on the mountain throw their waste into deep crevasses, but there were none around camp.

"Give me a break, you can't be serious. We can't do it in a crevasse around here?"

"Nope, none deep enough."

Craig looked over at me in distress. It was all I could do to keep from laughing.

"Look at it this way," I said. "If anyone asks, you can play the hero and say that you had to haul all our shit for a while."

"Terrific," Craig said, wrinkling his nose in disgust. "Load it on . . . but if any of that sludge leaks, I'm gonna be really, really pissed off!"

With shit and gear loaded, we began to climb. My muscles screamed in protest, having gotten too used to inactivity. It took awhile, but I finally managed to quell the revolt and get all my body parts working together.

We arrived at a crevasse field and Robert announced a brief break so that he and Craig could dump the latrine bag. Craig unharnessed himself and turned around to pick up the bag.

"Oh, you've got to be kidding me. I can't believe this shit." Craig dropped down to his knees and looked skyward, clasping his hands over his head.

Curious, I peered over at Craig's sled and saw the cause of his frustration. His worst nightmare had come true—the latrine bag had ruptured. A foul-smelling slush coated the inside of his sled. While feeling sorry for Craig, I felt extremely grateful Robert hadn't asked me to haul the latrine bag. I struggled to contain a wave of giggles for fear of getting belted by Craig—something I would have deserved.

Once the bag had been jettisoned, Craig set about scrubbing his sled with snow, muttering under his breath the entire time. He was not a happy camper, so I kept my distance.

During the final push to our new camp, we passed John Roskelley and Jim Wickwire, also on their way up Denali, though comfortably kicked back and resting for the moment.

"Lovely day for a stroll, don't you think?" Roskelley, world-class mountaineer and humorist.

At 11,000 feet, we cached our gear and then sat to admire the view before heading back down. Ahead of us I could see the Korean team working its way up. Robert was gazing at the Koreans, too.

"Those Koreans . . . they live to climb, but they can be a strange lot."

I raised my eyebrows and moved closer to Robert.

"Saw one of them stab a Sherpa once, simply because the Sherpa had refused to do something the Korean wanted him to do." Robert had a faraway look. "Stabbing a Sherpa. Makes no sense. They're the most gentle people on earth."

Robert hadn't mentioned what the Sherpa had refused to do, and I wasn't about to ask. I turned away and looked back down the mountain. I could see the German team below us, nine dots surrounding the Technicolor guide suit. Robert had shifted his stare from the Koreans to the Germans.

"Idiots!"

"Why?"

"Look where they're sitting."

I looked more closely and saw what Robert was getting at. The entire German team was lounging around and having lunch on top of a snow bridge. They seemed unaware that at any moment, the bridge could collapse, hurling all of them to their deaths. Climbing a mountain of this caliber requires generous portions of skill and a spoonful or two of luck. Unfortunately, as the Germans were proving, some teams rely too heavily on Lady Luck to fill up a plate empty of skill. I prayed that their luck held, for their sake.

We made it back down to our camp at 9,500 feet just as another wave of wind and snow slammed into us. Snow was falling so hard that we were obliged to climb out and knock the accumulation off our tent every few minutes. The wind-driven snow was so blinding that even the simple task of ducking outside the tent for a minute of shoveling required full battle dress and goggles.

Robert tried repeatedly to call for a weather update on the radio, but static was the only sound we heard. The temperature plummeted as did our spirits. It looked as if we were in for a long night.

{4} POCKET LINT OF THE GODS

—◆—

Day seven on the mountain

Sunlight filtered into the tent, a repeat of yesterday morning with one critical difference—*cold*. The sun's rays had no effect on the frost feathers coating the tent. My little hand-held thermometer registered 0 degrees inside our tent. Grateful that the storm of the night before had blown over, I wriggled over to the tent door and stuck my head out. Not a cloud in sight, except for the plume off the summit, indicating very high winds above.

"Well?"

"Sunny and cold and if you don't like the weather, move."

"And I wanted to go to Maui instead—imagine that. You go ahead and get dressed 'cause I'm milking all the warmth I can get out of this bag." Craig snuggled farther down into his bag, hiding from the day.

"We could flip for it?"

"Nope . . . you're already up anyway."

I sighed. Reaching for my bowl, I began to scrape the frost off the ceiling of the tent. No sense in dressing in a snow shower, which is what would happen if I kept bumping and rubbing the tent ceiling without first scraping. Reaching for my sunblock, my fingers found only a frozen tube. Terrific. I stuffed the icy plastic package into my sleeping bag next to my skin so that it would thaw.

"All right!" bellowed Robert. "Who's been walking around out here in the bird slippers?"

I looked at Craig and we both cracked up.

"Bird slippers? Whaddya mean bird slippers?" Randy yelled from the next tent.

"Well, either someone has been wearing bird slippers around out here or a mighty big bird has decided to have breakfast . . . our treat, apparently." Robert had a marvelous way of understatement.

"Let's kill the mother and eat him for breakfast," cried Randy.

We had seen ravens circling our camp whenever the weather cleared. They ranged in size from huge to absolutely humongous and had, apparently, located the food cache we had buried under the snow to ward off such raids. Their telltale footprints were dotted all around the cache. The feathered perpetrators had not only spotted the cache from the wands that marked it, but had somehow moved ice blocks, burrowed into the snow, and dragged out some packets of oatmeal. They'd also demonstrated a proclivity for ramen noodles. It was apparent that these birds, ordinarily not known for selective eating habits, had some culinary restrictions. Even a consummate scavenger such as the raven turned up its nose at retorts.

"They ate the best and left the rest," said Randy.

"Well, they didn't get everything," said Win. "Breakfast is on, so eat up and eat hearty. We've got a full day ahead."

I bit into a Pop Tart and cradled a hot cup of cocoa and a bowl of oatmeal. Simple foods, but oh so good!

"You know, Ruth Anne, I was standing in the room when Pete called you to say he'd gotten a permit for Everest and invited you to go."

I gazed at Win. That seemed so long ago, yet only a year had passed. "That's why I'm here . . . to gain experience for an Everest attempt."

"You don't want to go to Everest," chimed in Robert, speaking past mouthfuls of oatmeal. "Too much garbage, too many people, and it takes too damn long to climb. Nah, you should set your sights on Cho Oyu. It's still plenty high—27,000 feet, the seventh-highest in the world."

"Why Cho Oyu and not Everest?" Robert had been on Everest so I respected his opinion since I knew none of it was sour grapes.

"It's a shorter time span of your life to get up, only two months in fact. You'll see less people and the scenery . . . Oh, the scenery is incredible! You'll have views of Everest all the way up." Robert was actually showing a bit of passion. "I hope to do it in a couple of years."

"No crowds and great scenery? Sounds great. . . . Count me in."

Robert smiled as he got up to ready himself for the day's climb. "Besides, Pete's permit is for the post-monsoon season. You don't want to go then. That would put you approaching the summit as winter moved in and you're more likely to get stormed off. Better time to climb Everest, if it's something you still want to do, is in the spring, pre-monsoon. That way, the seasonal temperatures are warming as you climb and the weather is more stable."

Our little breakfast party broke up as we wandered back to our tents to begin the task of striking camp. Packs and sleds had to be loaded for the next carry, up to 11,000 feet where we had cached gear and food the day before. I finished loading up in short order, as did Randy.

"Hey, Ruth Anne? Randy?" Robert was summoning us. "We've got to crevasse another bag from the latrine so I want you two to rope up with me and help drag it across the snowfield to that crevasse field over there."

I looked to the north and could just make out the beginning of the field about a half mile distant. Our route took us in the same direction as the fractures, rather than across them as we had been doing yesterday when making our way up the mountain. That fact necessitated we abandon single-file hiking and resort to spreading out three abreast. That way, if one plunged through the snowy crust, we wouldn't all go down.

"This one'll do," motioned Robert.

The crevasse was a monster with jagged white teeth and a dark, black gullet. I hoped it had more of an appetite for latrine bags than humans. Robert worked himself to the edge, with me right behind ready to stop his fall, and heaved the bag out into space.

"Awww, shit!" Robert peered into the crevasse and shook his head in disgust. "I'm going to have to hang over the edge— belay me, Ruth Anne. The bag's hung up on a block of ice partway down and looks like crap . . . as well it should, I guess."

I laughed. Sinking my ice ax into the snow, I prepared to

hold Robert securely. He hung precariously over the lip and swung his ice ax in huge arcs, shattering snow and ice in an attempt to dislodge the ice block and the bag. All this just for a bag of shit. Fortunately, success came quickly and without incident. We hustled back to camp to load up and begin the next leg of our journey.

By ten A.M., under sunny skies and with a light breeze stirring the snow, we set out on snowshoes to move to Camp IV and 11,000 feet. I felt encumbered by my clothes and my waist harness was draped with hardware—carabiners, rescue pulleys, ascenders. Each crunch of snow underfoot was accompanied by the clink and clank of metal.

And the chain gang marched upward.

Exhausted, our crew reached Camp IV without incident. Robert had selected a breathtaking spot that sat adjacent to an aqua-colored icefall that spilled into an enormous crevasse. Sweeping views of the surrounding glaciers and mountains spread out before us.

"There's no doubt in my mind at all," Paul commented to no one in particular as he unfurled his tent, "this lot here definitely commands more on the real-estate market on the weight of its crevasse overlook alone."

"Maybe, but you'd best think about selling now while the weather looks good," fired back Randy. "I mean, the first sign of bad weather and all your prospective clients are going to hightail it down the mountain to the nearest Club Med."

With the sun beating down overhead, we had gone from subzero to almost balmy, and our mood soared to match. We were finally drying out and warming up.

That night, the temperatures took a nosedive—an expected occurrence as we moved higher up the mountain. Lying awake in my sleeping bag, struggling to stay warm, I listened to the glacier creak and groan underneath our tent. Perhaps there was a good reason why no one was camped on this prime bit of real estate we dubbed the "scenic crevasse overlook." The sounds took on an almost subterranean echo, as if the creaks, snaps, and groans were bouncing around in open space instead of passing through solid ice.

"Craig?"

"Yeah."

"You hearing what I'm hearing?"

"Oh yeah . . . Robert says it's caused by the glacier moving and settling under us. I find that rather unsettling myself."

"Yeah, me too."

I squeezed my eyes shut and tried to find sleep.

SUNDAY, MAY 10
Day eight on the mountain

Our sunny weather window was holding. Before ducking out of the tent to face the day, I ran my fingers gently over the raw and blistered flesh that once were soft lips and a smooth nose.

"Well, that seals it—my Revlon contract just went up in smoke."

"Yeah, riiiight . . . you might want to think about a promo for medicated lip balm at this point." Craig grinned broadly and then winced as his own lips reminded him that smiling came with a price—more cracking and bleeding.

With a bandanna wrapped tightly around my face to shield the sun's intensity, I began what would be our team's toughest carry thus far—from 11,000 to 13,500 feet.

Our route took us up a wall rising 1,000 feet above camp and onto an even steeper face above. The climbing was punishing work and slow going in crampons. With one step I was struggling to maintain a precarious balance on blue ice and with the next I was plunging up to my knees in snowdrifts. My sled would bounce along behind me, snagging just enough to keep me on edge. Traverses (climbing by hiking a more diagonal line, or a series of reversing and linked diagonal lines, across a steep slope) were the worst. During a traverse, gravity would pull the sled down the mountain, torquing my waist painfully and threatening to pull me off my feet at each step.

I was struggling up a particularly dangerous section of blue ice, the wall right beneath Windy Corner when Paul cried out.

"Hey, hold on guys," he pleaded. "Hang on a second."

I turned around to look at Paul, who was behind me on the rope. There, beneath one of his feet, lay pieces of one of his borrowed crampons. We were standing on the steepest, most exposed section of our climb so far and Paul was stuck with half a tread. I should have photographed it because it was all too unreal to believe.

"Oh man. I must not have adjusted them properly or something."

Yeah, no shit! I thought to myself.

Robert turned.

"Problem?"

"Ahh, yeah, yeah I've got a problem. One of my crampons came off. I need to stop here and put it back on."

"Not a chance!" Robert commanded. "When we get out of this section, then you can put it back on. For now, pick it up and carry it. You'll have to make do with one crampon."

Wonderful. I was regretting that Paul was right behind me on the rope; that he was the least surefooted of the team; and that now he had only one crampon. It suddenly occurred to me that I should try to get a message to my husband that I loved him more than ever—now that the risks had just doubled for me.

We reached Windy Corner safely and stopped for a break so Paul could fix his crampon. On close inspection, Robert determined that he had put the damn thing together wrong in the first place. That's what he got for using borrowed gear he hadn't even inspected before reaching the mountain.

Paul fumbled with the parts, struggling to assemble them in the cold. We just stared. No one smiled. No one spoke. Paul had screwed up and he knew it. His mistake could have cost us all a lot more than a mere delay.

"God, I'm sorry. I'm so sorry. Please, I'm trying, really trying here," Paul wailed.

"You gotta do more than try," I muttered under my breath.

I took a swig from my water bottle and replaced the lid. Before tucking it back into my parka, I went for one more sip, but the lid had frozen. I looked at Craig who was gazing back at me with wide eyes.

"Damn, now that's cold!" he said in mock horror.

"You're telling me! It froze in just seconds." I had to resort to hammering the lid with my ice ax to break it loose.

That night, back at our camp, we managed to get the radio working just long enough to hear a static-filled weather report from the park ranger. He was forecasting a huge storm blowing in from the Bering Strait and expected it to slam into Denali— 50-mile-per-hour winds and blowing snow above 14,000 feet, 25-to-30-mile-per-hour winds below 14,000 feet.

"So what else is new," remarked Vern glumly.

"Sounds like more of the same to me," agreed Jack.

"I do *not* want to spend another minute in the tent," whined Vern. "Someone needs to get injured or sick so we can get off of this mountain—kidding, of course." Vern looked up and managed a smile.

"Maybe we should just dial 911," quipped Randy, always quick with a one-liner.

"Before or after we toss one of us into a crevasse?" Craig was grinning broadly and looking right at Paul.

There was no question we were all getting antsy. This on-again, off-again weather pattern was cramping our climbing style and making it seem as though a summit attempt, if one came at all, might not happen for weeks—after all our food had run out. I, for one, was not the least bit excited about the prospect of having to hunker down in a cramped tent to ride out another weather front.

"Okay, I know the thought of another storm is not exactly cause for celebration; however, this is normal on Denali," said Robert calmly. "The best thing for us to do is move camp up to

14,000 feet tomorrow. That'll put us in a relatively protected area from the winds and it'll be a great place to weather out any Denali storm—much safer than here. On top of that, from 14,000 feet, we'll be well situated for a summit bid when the weather does break."

That sealed it. We weren't going to be getting off this mountain anytime soon. Robert's tone of voice and his announcement that we were going to go up to "weather" the storm made me feel as if we were going to war, not climbing a mountain. Then again, maybe we were in a war—with our emotions.

I awakened feeling very cramped. It took a few seconds, but soon I realized that the source of my dilemma was the tent's angle. Somehow, when Craig and I had pitched our tent, we had done so on a slight slope that had apparently been made worse by our crawling into and out of the tent during the day. Now, because of the slope, my nylon sleeping bag was acting like a sled and had deposited me in a heap at the foot of the tent. Not wanting to awaken Craig, I struggled to inch, worm, and claw my way back to the top of the tent where I lay back and tried to find sleep again.

A few minutes passed and then Craig, now at the bottom of our indoor luge run and not wanting to disturb me, went through the same gyrations, cursing quietly under his breath. We alternated sliding, slithering, then sleeping until, as fate would have it, we bumped heads while trying to be quiet enough not to disturb the other.

Rubbing my head, I looked at Craig and promptly burst out laughing.

"Gravity sure is a bitch, isn't it?" Craig said with tears streaming down his face.

"Yup. Maybe we should tie into a safety rope to keep from sliding?"

"Maybe we should have leveled the damn floor before pitching the tent!"

"Now there's an idea! While one could view sliding up and down as a form of exercise, I'd rather be spending my time waiting for a storm to break playing cards or sleeping. We *will* make sure the floor is level tomorrow."

"That's for sure!" Craig echoed. "Can you imagine having to hang out on a sloping floor for, say, four to five days and nights?"

I shuddered as I imagined repeating our mistake tomorrow at 14,000 feet—it would mean no rest for the weary, that's for sure.

"What do you think, four to five days from 14,000 feet to make the summit?" Craig continued.

"Yeah, if we're lucky and the weather clears. If we're not, it's going to be one long vacation. I can't think of anything worse."

"I can," said Craig moaning. "Making the summit with no food to spare and then getting back to basecamp but being unable to call in the planes because of weather."

I thought about it for a minute. No food. Totally exhausted. Nothing to do but wait. Total boredom. "Oh god, don't even think it! That would be a fate worse than death!"

MONDAY, MAY 11
Day nine on the mountain

Pure, unadulterated PAIN! If Hell has a frozen wasteland, then I had been hiking in it and through it for the last several hours. We had awakened in the middle of a storm, broken camp in the middle of a storm, and were now trying to climb up the mountain in the middle of a storm in a desperate race to get to Camp V and sheltered ground—3,000 feet above. My crampons would alternately scratch and scrape on blue ice and then plunge and disappear into thigh-deep drifts—drifts so deep they swallowed my leg and my momentum, stopping me so suddenly the weight of my pack would keep going, threatening to slam my face into the snow each time. My back muscles were screaming as they struggled to keep my body from torquing around as the 60-mile-per-hour wind grabbed at my pack, trying to twist and tear it from my back. At times, it felt as if the wind's icy fingers were trying to rip me apart. I had a sharp stabbing pain in my neck and a hot fire burning out of control in my upper shoulders, torso, and stomach. I would have screamed if I'd had the energy, not that it would have done any good or even been heard.

My pulse pounded in my temples and in my throat. Despite the raging winds, my ears remained sheltered in the cold deafness of my parka's hood, forced to listen to my own hoarse and heavy breathing. I could see nothing, feel nothing, other than my pain. As the minutes wore on, I managed to obtain a somewhat detached sense of reality as I slipped further and further into a mindless, pain-filled climbing rhythm—step, stumble, fight the sled, lean, step, brace against the wind, lurch, step, fight the sled, step, stumble . . .

Everything began to happen in slow motion. I felt as though I were suspended in milky water fighting against a very strong current and getting nowhere. Every now and then, I would watch in perverse fascination as the blackness of a deep crevasse would appear between my steps—though I couldn't really see them, I was somehow stepping over them. Strange. I wondered how Robert was managing to see anything at all. All I could focus on was the rope running from my harness onto the ground and disappearing into a white nothingness in front of me, connected somewhere up ahead to Robert. He left no footprints for me to follow . . . they were simply filling so quickly with snow. Even mine disappeared almost as soon as I lifted my feet. Each step I took became a step alone, just me, following a rope into who-knows-where.

"The only difference between me and a madman is that I'm not mad." I pondered Salvador Dalí's words as they echoed around the chambers of my mind. Climbing up the mountain in this weather seemed to be a mad proposition, and yet I knew I wasn't mad—at least I didn't think I was, and perhaps that made all the difference. What I was, was committed to climbing mountains, and as long as it didn't get me committed, I planned to keep at it a very long time.

A shadow appeared ahead of me on the rope, almost before I realized the rope had stopped moving and I was about to run over Robert.

"What's up?!" I yelled over the howl of the wind.

"Nothing's up. . . . We're here. The ice appears level and solid, so we set up camp," said Robert matter-of-factly. The climb up in near-blinding conditions was just another walk in the park for him. I had the sense he'd often seen weather like this, and perhaps far worse.

Although we were tired and cold, there would be no rest until ice walls were constructed and the tents pitched. We unroped and lined up our sleds next to one another with our packs lashed to them.

Franklin, bless his heart, began to direct traffic—not in a commanding way, but by offering suggestions and by example. A quiet man at all other times, every camp became a city-in-planning for him, and we all benefited from his energy and engineering know-how.

Some of us got down on our hands and knees and began cutting ice squares with the saws. As soon as a piece was cut, another on the team would jump in with a shovel, frequently Franklin, and pry the piece loose while the cutter would slide a few feet to one side and begin another block. We were a high-mountain assembly line—cutter to shovel to human forklift to construction worker. Slowly but surely, the walls rose to five feet high—creating a compound just high enough to break the wind and shelter a dome tent pitched within.

Vern, impatient with the building process, slipped away from the group and began to pitch his tent.

"You know, Vern, this would go a lot faster if you'd help out. . . . Besides, I don't think pitching the tent without the shelter walls is a good idea," yelled Franklin while prying yet another block loose.

"I'm just so damn cold and I want to get the tents up. . . . If I begin this now we'll be ahead of the game," fired back Vern.

"Suit yourself," replied Franklin, never really looking at Vern but instead focusing on prying another block loose.

"Oh *fuck*!" Vern screamed, barely audible over the wind.

I turned just in time to witness the first tent in orbit.

"I had that baby anchored, too! Oh God . . ." His voice trailed off as the tent climbed even higher, nearly twenty feet in the air, spinning fast like a giant beach ball being knocked about in a stadium at a football game.

Fortunately, after a short pursuit, the tent was tackled and subdued, its escape attempt thwarted by Robert and an equally quick-thinking Win.

"Look, I've seen winds up here rip apart tents. Do not pitch a tent until the ice walls are finished or you'll be without a tent and that will be the finish," admonished Robert, looking squarely at Vern who averted his stare.

I had no idea what Vern was thinking and I was equally amazed that he'd even managed to pitch the tent at all. Even with the sheltering walls, Craig and I had to repeatedly throw ourselves on our tent while we were pitching it just to keep it from beating too wildly in the wind and making good on an escape attempt.

With our tent up and secure, it occurred to me that someone should check on the gear that had been sitting off to the side, just to make sure everything was still there and secure. Since the others continued busily putting finishing touches on ice walls and pitching their tents, I beckoned to Craig and we wandered over to the sleds.

Craig stopped abruptly in his tracks, his face turned to the row of sleds. I followed his gaze and my eyes rested on Paul, sitting regally on the end of the last sled in line, munching happily on a candy bar.

Craig's face took on an angry color. "Dammit! Every time there is a tough job to do, he sneaks off to the side and watches."

To be honest, I hadn't really noticed until now. I bent over and began to dig out our rope coils, which were rapidly getting buried, and lay them on top of the sleds where we'd be able to find them later.

Craig continued to mutter to himself. "I'm used to working with a team, as a team and I'm sick and tired of having to pick up the slack."

"Then don't." The solution seemed simple to me. Each time someone slacks off and someone else covers for them, the slacker learns nothing and the person doing the extra work becomes exhausted and frustrated. "No one except you expects that much of you. You've got to pace yourself because you're going to need every ounce of energy later."

"Yeah, I know." Craig shrugged his shoulders and softened his glare somewhat. "It just pisses me off the way some people do that every damn time."

"You know, Craig, anger is a form of energy. Turn it into something positive and use it, but use it wisely."

Craig stared at me and nodded. "Thanks."

The subject was closed and we got back to work. There was a kitchen cave to dig. This was going to be no ordinary weather front, I could sense it. The snow was falling so fast that as I walked it covered each boot before I could lift it for my next step. The temperature felt as though it was falling almost as fast as the flakes—and we weren't even in the eye of the storm yet. The Mountain of Extremes was proving itself handily.

Like prisoners of war, we dug to escape our tormentor, the wind. It took many hours to excavate as we burrowed down eight feet beneath the surface. The roof above us was approximately two feet thick. The inside of the cave was twelve feet long, six feet wide, and five feet high. We fashioned a shelf at one end on which we placed the stoves for cooking. Directly above the stove, we drilled a hole approximately one foot wide through the ceiling. Above, we protected the opening with ice blocks. The threat of carbon monoxide poisoning, a common cause of fatalities among climbers, made our chimney construction all the more important. Finally, we carved sitting benches running the length of the two walls and storage holes above the benches for placing our mugs and food bags.

The cave was shelter, but only just. It had no ambience, unless very cramped quarters were your pleasure. Because the only light filtering in from the door opening was often obscured by the mass of humanity packed inside, we ate and drank in gloom. This was not such a bad thing. It was better not to have to see what we were eating in most cases. Since cold sinks, we had created an environment that was as cold if not colder than being outdoors. Foam pads to insulate your feet and butt were mandatory. The condensation from our breath and the steam from boiling water filled the cave, giving the appearance of a smoke-filled room. I hated that cave, we all did. That night, as we huddled in the ice cave sipping hot cocoa, Robert estimated that we would probably be weathered in for another four days or so.

"We'll play it safe," said Robert. "If all goes well, we'll be on our way up in four days. From here it'll take another three days to summit and then three days more to get all the way back down the mountain in time to catch a plane ride to Talkeetna."

Playing it safe was a comforting thought. At least here, at 14,000 feet, we were somewhat sheltered. The only catch to the plan was that our food cache, the one we had stashed yesterday, was now sitting about 1,000 feet below us and would have to be ferried up here sometime soon. It would not be a good thing to get so weathered in that we died of starvation only feet from our food. At least going down was easier than going up in some respects. From chatting with others trapped on this icy shelf, I learned that one team had decided to err on the side of recklessness and carried food and supplies up the mountain, to 16,000 feet—despite the impending weather onslaught. Now, they were cut off from their food and supplies, safely cached 2,000 feet above. I shuddered, half from the cold and half from the thought of heading back to my tent for another prolonged storm vigil. This was shaping up to be a very long climb indeed.

{5} WE'RE NOT IN KANSAS ANYMORE, TOTO

TUESDAY, MAY 12
Day ten on the mountain

I sat bolt upright, stirred from a fitful sleep by Craig turning over. As I recovered from the dizzying sensation of blood rushing from my head, I became acutely aware that my legs were numb from the knees down. This wasn't the kind of tingling numb you experience from not moving over long periods of time—I couldn't feel anything at all. There had been no warning, no expected chilling or trembling. Just a sense that since I could no longer feel my feet or the weight of the sleeping bag on them, something must be dreadfully wrong.

Fumbling with my zipper, I tore open my sleeping bag and ripped off my down booties and woolen socks. My lower legs were bone white and coated with a thin layer of ice, my feet yellow, my toes black and frozen solid. I was accustomed to seeing frozen flesh on others, even cadavers, though nothing prepared me for the sight of my own flesh, frozen and glistening. It seemed strangely curious that swaddled as I was in down, I was freezing to death on this mountain from the feet up. My toes, sparkling eerily in the translucent light of the tent, were glued together by the cold, leaving me no alternative but to pry them apart, one by one. It is a weird feeling to tug on a part of your body and not feel anything at all. I knew I had to do something to save myself and do it fast.

Forcing myself into action, I doubled up my sleeping bag, placing it underneath my body to further insulate me from the ice shelf our tent stood on. By pulling my feet underneath my buttocks, I began the painful task of trying to warm them with my body heat. I felt as though I were sitting on lumps of frozen meat. I struggled to stay warm and focused, even though the tent, continually lashed by the Arctic wind, snapped and shook violently as the bitter air cut through its walls. The paralyzing cold took my breath away, but it was the awful noise that began to unnerve me.

I may just as well have been sitting in a paper bag for all the protection the tent walls offered. Struggling to keep my feet under my body, I rummaged for my expedition parka and wrapped it tightly around the upper half of my body. As I grabbed the metal zipper tab to pull it closed, my skin stuck to it. Packaged head to toe in insulating down, I sat there, rocking back and forth, stunned and in disbelief . . . my mind racing in a confused whirl. What if Craig hadn't moved?

The thought of losing my toes to amputation was minor compared with the fear of what might have happened. It is a simple equation—if you don't stay warm, you die. There is no gray area here. Ever since childhood, I had demanded much of my body, and it had always delivered in the crunch. Subjecting my body to this brutal cold, however, may have been asking too much of it. My heart had simply failed to keep all of me warm. Worse yet, the chilled blood my heart was circulating through my frozen limbs could lead me down the path to hypothermia—

if I didn't thaw out fast. I wrestled with the thought that a more horrible fate than sacrificing my feet to frostbite would be an inability to get myself off this mountain. I had climbed up, and I was damn well going to climb back down if I had anything to say about it.

Assuming I could thaw out my feet, keeping them from refreezing was not going to be easy. When extended, my six-foot frame reached the width of the tent, forcing my feet to rest directly against the frigid side. The only solution would require assuming a fetal position—not an easy proposition with two adults crammed into a space the size of a twin bed, a situation we'd been forced into and were doing our best to manage.

Sitting silently, I glanced around the inside of the tent, which had begun to look like the inside of a deep freeze—one badly in need of defrosting. Ice crystals covered everything from ceiling to floor. Snowdrifts weighted against the outside walls, sagging them in on top of us, straining our frail structure, threatening to collapse it and bury us alive. A dim gray-green light diffused through the tent fabric in the few places not obscured by snow, creating an eerie scene that did nothing to instill a feeling of life, or of healing.

The comfort received at the sight of my few familiar possessions—my boots, clothes, and water bottle—was tempered with the realization that, like the inside of the tent and my feet underneath me, they, too, were frozen solid. Spotting my thermometer, I scraped through a thick crust of ice to confirm my fears. Like being drawn to gawk at a horrible accident, I didn't really want to know the temperature yet I felt compelled by a morbid curiosity to see the numbers and truth for myself. My ability to deny the obvious was quickly disintegrating. There, in black-and-white, was reality. The mercury held at below minus-20 Fahrenheit inside this icebox of nylon. I could only imagine how cold it was outside with the wind chill factored in. I was caught in my worst nightmare and it had only just begun.

On the other side of the thin nylon membrane, avalanches thundered down all around us—like mortars exploding—shaking the ground on impact. The wind roared through our tiny camp like a freight train, torquing our tents into unthinkable configurations. Even earplugs didn't muffle the sound. It was an audible assault you felt as much as heard. The relentless crashing and howling penetrated to the core of my soul, shaking and rattling my sanity.

Craig stirred, pulling me out of my funk and focusing me back on the present. Tuning in to my obvious discomfort, he became alarmed at my plight. Had the shoe been on the other foot, pun intended, I would have been alarmed, too. It is one thing to be cold and uncomfortable and entirely another to be trapped in a tent next to a teammate with frozen body parts. Craig needed me as much as I needed him if we were to have any hope of getting up and down this mountain in one piece. A shared tent is a shared fate. Any vestige of a sane world extended only as far as its nylon walls. We were very much alone with each other, the mountain, and our own mortality.

I tried to reassure him, but who was I kidding? I had always begun my climbs strong and come home shriveled and perhaps a little bit sore. Having to cope with frozen feet, however, was uncharted territory for me. I knew that I had to drink copious amounts of fluid to help not only with my frostbite, but also my acclimatizing to the altitude—sort of like a high-octane anti-freeze.

But to drink, I had to first thaw out my frozen water bottle. That meant shoving it inside my parka next to my skin until the ice thawed to a slushy consistency suitable for slurping. An ice cube down the shirt as a summertime prank brings laughter, but this, a tube of ice next to my skin in subzero temperatures, was a necessary and intentional misery.

Craig pushed his Gore-Tex bivi sack on me to put over my sleeping bag for extra warmth. While the sack would add a vital 10 degrees of thermal capacity to my sleeping bag, I couldn't take it. He'd lugged it up the mountain and besides, if both of us became crippled, we would be in a worse fix than we were in now. I insisted that he keep it. He insisted I take it. Chivalry won over logic and I accepted his generosity.

My heating efforts began to pay off as my feet began to tingle. Then there was pain, shooting through every fiber of my body like electrical shocks. Pain—a sign of life. A friend once noted that the key to mountaineering was "one's ability to endure pain." With success or failure in the sport of mountaineering hinging on health, weather, and mountain conditions, I was not continuing this climb on an optimistic note. So far, I had three strikes against me. The things we do to ourselves in the name of recreation.

I dreaded going outside, but I had no choice if I wanted to save my feet. Walking was going to be the only way to accelerate the thawing process. Besides, sitting on my feet for a prolonged period couldn't be doing great things for my circulation. Craig volunteered to act as human ballast in our tent–cum–mountain sailplane.

"There's no way I'm going out in this unless I absolutely have to," he asserted over the wind's violent roar. Craig had the luxury of a choice—I didn't.

Gearing up to brave the elements was no small task, and wrestling with clothing in such tight quarters required the agility of Houdini. The essential layers seemed endless. Over two pairs of long underwear went fleece, down, and Gore-Tex. My expedition parka, equivalent to half a sleeping bag, comprised the final layer. Gloves, overmitts, hat, and goggles topped off the ensemble. I was strangely thankful that my comatose feet never felt the boots that had frozen solid overnight.

I unzipped the tent door to face the onslaught, wincing before the full force of the storm as it swept in and covered us both with snow. I couldn't believe this was happening, that I was really going to go out in this violence, but I moved quickly out of the tent to minimize the inward thrust. Standing erect for the first time in many hours, the elements battered my unsteady body and I wobbled precariously on top of a pair of dead stumps.

There was no turning back. I had to walk to save my feet— to save me. As I stepped out, I had no idea what I was walking into. To leave the tent was to enter an unforgiving world of high-velocity blindness and deafening noise. The only thing distinguishing up from down was the force of gravity holding me unconvincingly to the ground—a force undermined and weakened by the power of the wind threatening to sweep me off my feet and hurl me down the mountain. I had become a willing participant in an exercise in violence, a mere speck of dust against the teeth of a savage Alaskan storm.

The wind-driven snow assaulted the bare skin of my face like so many pinpricks. It fell so fast that my footprints filled in immediately as I walked. The bitter-cold gusts seemed to come from all directions, which made sense considering our camp was in an enormous bowl. Though the immediate geography was now impossible to survey, a week earlier we had glimpsed this location from below. I knew that on three sides of us loomed 2,000- and 3,000-foot vertical walls of rock. Corralled by features shaped with the forces of nature—ridges, cliffs, and ripe avalanche chutes—camp sat in the middle of a Bermuda Triangle of ice and snow. It was a humbling place to be, especially in a whiteout.

Of course, "triangle" implies three sides, but this ice shelf on which I stood had a fourth, more ominous side, spilling off 6,000 feet and exposing a section of ice twenty stories thick. Our camp was on this moving, frozen slab and somewhere out there was the edge. As if tumbling blindly off the edge wasn't enough to deal with, I had to remain conscious of a more pressing and immediate danger lurking invisibly, here, just below the surface—crevasses.

Though only a few feet away, I could barely make out the four tents housing our team of ten. A few shadowy forms—like space walkers—floated in and out of view, moving in slow, deliberate motions. Despite being late in the morning, there was no hint of sun as the field of vision disappeared into a lead-gray void.

Leaning into the force of the wind, I stomped about as snow pelted me and froze to my face. I grabbed one of our shovels and began digging drifts from the side of our tent. Activity would help the thawing process and keep my mind occupied. In spite of the five-foot walls we had erected with ice blocks cut from the glacier, the accumulation of snow still threatened to bury us alive. I could hear Craig's muffled voice filter through the snow and wind, cheering me on from inside:

"Now this is more like it. Tent with the woman and have her do all the tough work. Keep it up, Ruth Anne, you're doing great!"

"Don't get too used to it," I yelled into a wind that tried to snatch my words away. "There's plenty more where this came from, just begging for you to take your turn."

I had to smile at his reference to me as "the woman." It was a distinction I had held on every other major peak as well. It didn't bother me. After all, it was part of the challenge that I had bought into, the mountain, the elements, and even being alone with this group of men. It was the different facets of the challenge that made the experience so intellectually consuming. I was glad he hadn't referred to me as the oldest, though. This climb was the first on which I ranked as the senior member of a team, an inevitability if you do this sport long enough. What a lousy forty-fifth birthday present this was shaping up to be. Forty-five years represented many fun tickets, but this wasn't turning out to be the E-ticket ride I had dreamed. We were weathered in and hadn't even hit the eye of the storm yet.

After digging out the tent, I decided to explore our compound. Hobbling about, grateful to be able to walk at all, I discovered that our team was not alone. We were part of a hastily erected international temporary village, surrounded by tents, ice-block walls, and snow caves from other teams on the mountain. I marveled at some of the elaborate structures equipped with courtyards, outdoor cooking platforms, and seating benches carved from ice. Some appeared as fortresses of snow—like giant sandcastles fashioned from a child's imagination. All flew the colors of their homeland—Germany, Holland, Switzerland, Italy, Korea, and two from the U.S.A. Snapping wildly in the frigid wind, flags from a variety of nationalities cordoned off a multinational team's camp—the United Nations of our little enclave high above the world. Seven teams stuck on an ice shelf with nowhere to run.

Just beyond the main cluster of camps stood a red, plastic-coated canvas tent, approximately ten by twelve feet, known as the "medical station." This temporary, Quonset-like hut housed a radio and limited medical supplies. A mountain ranger, who based out of a nearby tent, checked in there periodically. Under normal circumstances, the medical station was a gathering point of sorts, a place for socializing and swapping information and tales. There would be no socializing today—it was too damn cold and windy. The tent stood stoically, its door zipped shut and locked. I pondered the information sign that hung from its side:

9:30 A.M. weather forecast for 5/12/92
Predicted worst storm in 10 years
Winds up to 110 mph, (160 km)
Heavy snowfall on west slopes
WELCOME TO DENALI

Terrific! To think I was actually paying for this. This summit attempt was rapidly shaping up to become my longest self-inflicted wound. Other climbs had been mere strolls, but here, on Denali, every one of us huddled on this hunk of rock and ice was hostage to the dark side of mountaineering.

"I must be out of my mind," I muttered to no one but the wind.

My husband's words came back to haunt me, an admonition born of his concern that I had been seduced by a deadly allure. "Wait until you get caught up high in a really bad storm. That'll change your opinion of climbing." His words resounded through my mind, echoing in the wildness of the storm like a self-fulfilling prophecy.

I thumped about the medical station in a mood that was beginning to match the darkness of the storm. As I cursed the weather and the cold that numbed my bones, a Gore-Tex-clad, down-padded figure approached, his face recessed in the hood of his jacket like that of the Grim Reaper. Fortunately, the Grim Reaper doesn't wear a ranger's insignia, barely visible under a thick layer of rime frost.

He came within a few feet of me, allowing me to make out a blond beard and mustache, covered with icicles, protruding from below his goggles.

"What team are you with?" he yelled over the wind.

"I'm with Robert Link and Win Whittaker. We got here last night. My name's Ruth Anne." It was like trying to have a conversation at a heavy-metal rock concert while standing in front of a stack of speakers.

"Howdy, I'm Ron, the ranger up here. You guys have all

your people?" He seemed genuinely worried—who wouldn't be in a storm like this?

"Yeah, we're not going anywhere until this weather lifts . . . Why?"

"A party retreating from above reported spotting two bodies swinging from a tangle of ropes at 16,000 feet. We won't be able to check it out until things improve, so I'm taking a head count."

A grisly image sprang into my mind—an image of broken, twisted, mangled corpses, beating against the rock like perpetual pendulums of death. I struggled to insulate myself mentally, knowing in my heart that their mistake wouldn't be our mistake, therefore their fate wouldn't be ours. It was an unconvincing burst of logic amid a stormy sea of emotion. I had witnessed such sights before. I didn't need to relive them—not here, where it was neither safe nor entertaining to scare oneself. My own experience with my feet was tangible fear enough. As I had learned from other incidents on other mountains, I had to cloak my emotions in an iron-clad armor of cold steel.

"Any idea who?" I managed tersely.

"Yeah, I'm pretty sure it's a couple of Italian guys who checked in here a few days ago. They planned to blitz the Cassin ridge in two or three days."

My stomach tightened. They were the apparently very experienced mountaineers whom I'd seen parading around basecamp only days earlier with their Italian flare. They dressed in fluorescent, insulated bodysuits covered with sponsorship patches, like race-car drivers. I remembered joking that fluorescent clothing was good for only one thing—locating a body. Little did I dream . . .

I told Ron that we had seen them in basecamp, that they appeared flashy.

He shook his head and looked away, toward what, I don't know. "They were both expert alpinists, but when I tried to warn them about the weather here, they just laughed. They were traveling light and fast—didn't have a tent or even a shovel for digging a snow cave. Their entire load could have fit in a day pack. Probably they were caught off-guard by the sudden impact of the storm and blown from the ridge above."

Blown from the ridge, tumbling like two leaves before an autumn breeze—except it was summer and this wind resembled a hurricane more than a breeze. I had to push the thought back—get off this discussion of bodies. The Italians should have known better, plain and simple. Experience means caution and caution means knowing when to quit. Doors began slamming shut in my mind, protecting me against the rapidly mounting odds. If I was to survive, I had to be mentally invincible— hard as steel, bulletproof. That meant changing the subject fast. Talk about anything but bodies—weather, we could talk about weather.

"I can't imagine being any higher in this. We were at 12,000 feet yesterday when it hit. I hadn't seen anything like it—blue sky one minute, and a full-blown blizzard the next. No warning. Nothing."

Perhaps he sensed the conversation was over or that there was no point in discussing death further. Turning to stomp off into the storm and continue his head count, Ron yelled, "We haven't seen the worst of it yet. I don't have a good feeling. I won't spend lives to save lives. We are in for a really weird time up here."

The snowy veil closed in around him, leaving me standing alone once again, buffeted by the elements and absorbing this new shock to my system. I struggled to keep my mind from spinning out of control. A human life seemed like a lot to pay just to climb a mountain. What was the point if you didn't come back? In fact, was there really a point if you did? I'd had narrow escapes before, but this mountain was cutting dangerously close to my soul. Mountaineering, as I knew it, was about living—not beating death. Longevity translated into safety.

An explosion of wind snapped me from my stupor. I had to lunge forward to keep from being knocked backward and off my feet. White death swirled in a nebulous world where sky merged into the ground. The weather's sudden force urged me to return to the relative security of our tent.

With my arm in front of my face, shielding against the stinging snow, I struggled back. The light was flat, shadowless, cold, and gray. Everything began to look the same. Visually, nothing made sense. I was getting disoriented and had to fight to keep from panicking.

Methodically I worked my way through the camps, hopscotching from one to the next only when I could visually lock on to a target. I covered the area, trying to get a feel for its dimension. I passed by the same camps a second and third time. In the swirling snow, I had lost all sense of direction. For all I knew, I was moving farther away from our tents and closer to the edge of that 6,000-foot drop—the fourth wicked edge to this frigid Bermuda Triangle.

No one was out—as if that should have been a surprise. I shouldn't be out anymore, either, but in a way I was grateful for the solitude. I felt foolish, embarrassed. Wandering aimlessly in such hostile conditions could give the appearance of having gone mad from cold or lack of oxygen. Maybe I had and just didn't realize it.

I dug through the layers for my watch, searching for any information to help illuminate the problem. I had been retracing my aimless path for forty-five minutes . . . an eternity. I was ready to be "home."

The only way to find our tents was to break this looping cycle I was wandering in. The tents had to lie in another direction—but in which direction did I dare to venture? I chose a new approach, zigzagging between camps, offering a chance to sweep the terrain in a different pattern.

I stumbled, catching myself in time to keep from falling into the entrance of another team's ice cave. It was as though the ground had opened up in front of me. I tried to console myself. At least it wasn't a crevasse and, if I fell and broke my leg, I wouldn't be able to feel it anyway. I cracked a smile even though I danced around the raw edges of terror.

The snow, blowing sideways now, scoured my face. The only thing I hadn't done was smack facefirst into an ice-block wall—something I now fully expected to do. It had happened to me once before on another trip, while skiing in a whiteout, planting my head and ski tips into a drift of snow while still standing upright. That had been comical. This was not.

A shadow moved. A closer inspection revealed it was Craig, out repairing the ice-block walls, a white-on-white camouflage obscuring our orange tents. No doubt I'd passed within a few yards of this wall while circling blindly. My heart pounded in my chest as the tension and fears I had been coping with evaporated in relief. I wanted to hug him.

Craig stopped working and leaned on his shovel. "Welcome home, stranger. I was beginning to worry about you."

"I was beginning to worry about me, too. I got lost."

"Perhaps it would be wiser if we travel in tandem—until we get the lay of the land here. Having two bodies to look for will make us easier to find anyway," he added with a chuckle.

Two bodies . . . The hideous image of the Italians, medallions of death hanging from the mountain, flashed back through my mind again. I thought it best not to mention it just yet to Craig—if I couldn't shield myself, I could at least shield him.

"How are the feet?" asked Craig, without really looking my way. I think Craig sensed I knew something that perhaps he didn't want to know.

"I can still walk, but it's hard staying balanced with no sensation in my feet. I'll have to get used to it, I guess. I saw the ranger. He said this storm was going to get a lot worse before it gets better."

Craig nodded silently as I picked up a shovel to make ready for the siege.

WEDNESDAY, MAY 13
Day eleven on the mountain

One-hundred-mile-per-hour winds slammed into our little camp with horrific force. It's amazing that any of our tents remained standing, but they did, *thank God*. Last night was misery relived. The sweet pleasure of a simple cup of hot chocolate overloaded my bladder, forcing me up and leaving me cursing my body for the untimely need. Why couldn't the call of nature just go unanswered until after the frenzy subsided? Grabbing at the zipper tab on the tent door, my fingers stuck to the metal like a kid's tongue to a screen door on a winter's day dare. At this rate, I wasn't going to have much skin left.

Once outside, I struggled to shuffle ten feet before looking over my shoulder and realizing that the tents had disappeared from view in the blowing snow. A scream for help would have gone unheard over the roar of the wind. I could see the headlines now, "Mountaineering Woman Dies While Peeing." They would find me after the storm abated, frozen in mid-squat—not a pretty thought.

Fortunately, mountaineering clothing comes designed for function, not fashion. The pants feature a rear drop flap, rather like the traditional red long johns worn by pioneers in the late 1800s. The intent behind the drop flap was to minimize exposure, which it did, to an extent. Up here, where frostbite happens in seconds, the flap setup was a lifesaver. Nevertheless, the zippers had a nasty tendency to freeze up in the down position leaving no alternative but to drop mittens and struggle barehanded to shut out the cold rushing in the back door. It was a simple matter of risking your fingers to frostbite to save your butt.

I retraced my steps carefully, gratefully returning to the relative sanctuary of my nylon-shielded world. From now on, I vowed to resort to a pee bottle like the men, a tricky maneuver, but then my priorities had definitely shifted. This particular activity was not worth repeating outdoors.

"So, this is our weather window?" Craig grumbled.

Talk of a break in the low-pressure system had circulated but, of course, the break never materialized. Robert had said earlier that this was rapidly approaching the worst weather he'd ever seen. Having nothing to compare it to, I didn't doubt him. The storm had apparently enveloped the mountain. Going either up or down was no longer an option. Here we were camped and here we would stay.

I was increasingly glad for Craig's company. We shared a similar trait of remaining calm when confronted with danger and crisis and there was plenty of both surrounding us now. We intended to go home not only with our lives, but with all of our body parts intact and in working order. Too often, climbers become victims of their own confidence or fear. One can never know too much or listen too closely. There needs to be a consonance with the mountain while respecting what the elements have to say—today the elements were shrieking.

There was nothing to do but wait out the storm. Minutes ticked by slowly in the tent. We lay there listening to the sound—you could never escape the sound. I wondered if we'd have any eardrums left after this. The wind, when it gusted, was almost explosive, receding to a loud roar before shattering violently into our camp again, and again, and again. My heartbeat surged and subsided with the ebb of the wind and the thunder of nearby avalanches.

Craig and I discussed the theory that we are all born with a preprogrammed number of heartbeats. We wondered, if the theory were true, whether the present experience was shaving years off of our lives with each adrenaline-induced surge of concern. And, did it really matter? Heartbeat at rest, 52. Heartbeat after a nearby avalanche, 124.

The storm was taking its toll on more than our nerves. We had arrived in camp with just enough food for one more day, leaving the rest below, cached at 13,000 feet. Mountaineering, in its most basic terms, is going up and down a mountain in a series of calculated and well-timed moves. You start at the bottom of a mountain with a pile of gear and food that resembles a mini-mountain itself. Day by day, the team works its way up the route, first establishing a camp, then going down and back up relaying food and gear to that camp. The process repeats itself with higher camps and more relays until the peak is reached or the team retreats. Now, pinned at 14,000 feet, our efficient machine was stalled and running out of time, food, and fuel.

Low fuel meant keeping water bottles next to our skin all day and night to prevent them from freezing. Cuddling with a plastic bottle of slush is far from comfortable, but drinking the thick liquid is excruciating. Drinking was critical to our survival on this mountain. We drank to stay alive, to prevent frostbite, and to minimize the potential effects of altitude. In drinking to survive, we subjected ourselves to ingesting a numbing cold that assaulted the body with stomach cramps and headaches, like chugging down a Slurpie or eating ice cream too quickly.

Keeping a bottle of water next to my skin all day long was risky as well. While a wet bed at home is merely uncomfortable,

The climbing team is flown by bush pilots into
Kahiltna Base camp on May 3, 1992.

Climbers carry sixty-pound packs and drag sleds loaded with
fifty pounds of gear as they move up the Kahiltna Glacier.

Camp II at elevation 8,000 feet. Tents are secured by walls of ice blocks cut from the glacier. Summit of McKinley is visible (white arrow) as well as the ice shelf at 14,000 feet (black arrow).

Camp II at 8,000 feet. Weather deteriorates over the summit as a deadly lenticular cloud cap forms.

The team works its way between storms from Camp III at 9,500 feet to Camp IV at 11,000 feet.

Negotiating a crevasse on the glacier.

View from within a sixty-foot-deep crevasse.

Camp IV
at 11,000 feet.

Tent in snow
at 14,000 feet.

Below: Storage tent adjacent to medical station. Alex Von Bergen, a forty-two-year-old Swiss mountain guide, dies in camp at 14,000 feet and is placed in a body bag (far right). The body remains in camp for the duration of the storm.

The medical station is lashed by ground blizzards as the storm abates.

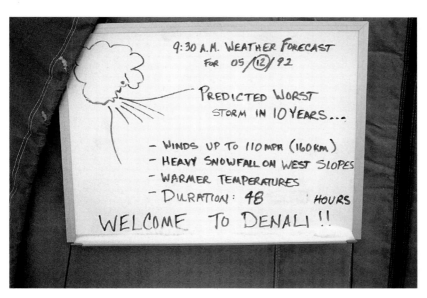

9:30 A.M. WEATHER FORECAST
FOR 05/12/92

PREDICTED WORST
STORM IN 10 YEARS...

- WINDS UP TO 110 MPH (160 KM)
- HEAVY SNOWFALL ON WEST SLOPES
- WARMER TEMPERATURES
- DURATION: 48 HOURS
WELCOME TO DENALI !!

Weather report posted on medical station located
14,000 feet up Mt. McKinley, in Alaska.

Tents and ice walls
in Camp V at
14,000 feet.

View of the ice
shelf and camp
(arrow) at 14,000
feet from 17,200
feet. Mt. Foraker
and the Kahiltna
Glacier are visible
in the background.

After twenty-one days on the mountain the team approaches the top along the summit ridge.

View from the summit as climber approaches. The knife ridge drops off to the left 9,000 vertical feet—one of the single greatest plunges on earth—to the glaciers below.

After spending scarcely twenty minutes on top, the team retreats the summit ridge and makes its way back to high camp.

The author on the summit of Mt. McKinley at 7:00 P.M.,
May 23, 1992.

here on the mountain it can mean death. As I lay there hour after hour, staring mindlessly at the snapping fabric of our tent and hugging my water bottle, I couldn't shake the thought of the climber on K2 whose feet had frozen when his bottle leaked. He ultimately lost his feet, but managed to escape with his life. I thought of my feet, and then of the water bottle, then the climber, and then the storm. The cold sheen of my emotional armor, so necessary to protect me on this mountainside, was beginning to show signs of rust.

There was an upside to all this snow and wind. It gave Craig and me something constructive to do. Staying active took our minds off the risks, monotony, and claustrophobia of hanging out in a nylon shelter that, at times, assumed the ambience of a frozen sarcophagus. Every so often, because of the snowdrifts that threatened to entomb us on the mountain until the next thaw, we were forced outside to dig out the tent and bolster the snow-wall fortifications.

A lone mountaineer, apparently delirious from altitude, staggered through camp like a Saturday-night drunk with his boots unbuckled and dragging a sled, while Craig and I struggled to shovel and move snow from around our tent. He kept right on going, never looking up and never asking for help. He was heading toward the medical tent. We didn't try to stop him or offer assistance because there wasn't anything that we could do. You cannot act like Mother Teresa on the mountain and expect to live. The best thing mountaineers can do for others is to take care of themselves.

Perhaps it is a harsh reality, but there is no denying that being prepared is the security blanket of the successful mountaineer, success being measured in increments of life and death. Ignorance is sometimes bliss, but it can be a deadly liability in the mountains. Forget where you are and let down your guard, even for a minute, and the mountain may claim you forever. Worse, individuals such as the one stumbling through our camp were liabilities not only to themselves but to others. They exact a costly toll on the strained resources and strength of everyone with whom they come in contact, more so if a rescue is required.

I thought back to my January 1990 climb on Aconcagua in South America when our team came across a solo mountaineer while we were approaching the summit. He was delirious, his clothing shredded from a recent fall, and yet he insisted on continuing up despite our adamant demands that he turn back. I never knew if he succeeded—neither did he, I'm sure.

Those who do not listen to the mountain, or to themselves, are accidents waiting to happen. I gazed up to where I thought the peak might lie through the swirling snow, and wondered about the Korean team I had watched starting up the ridge yesterday, tiny dots struggling to stand upright against the force of the wind. Despite the obvious severity of the weather and the stern warning from the ranger and the medical-tent message board, they had elected to proceed upward and onto the exposed Cassin ridge where they were certain to be subjected to the worst any storm could throw at them. It was a kamikaze mentality—a disaster in the making.

My mind drifted back to 8,000 feet when I had commented, almost casually, as we observed the Korean team placing their ice-block walls near our second camp, "Watch them, Craig, I

guarantee it will be exciting, but don't get anywhere near them."
I had forecast trouble ten days before, and now, seeing it come
to life before my eyes scared me. The Koreans were dead and I
knew it.

Standing next to the tent, shoveling shoulder-to-shoulder
with Craig, I began to sense that something horrific was about
to unfold on this mountain—and I was going to be a captive
witness.

The rumor mill circulating among the camps buzzed that
another storm front, larger than the first, was preparing to slam
into us at any moment. Dreading a return to the confines of the
tent, I used the weather rumor as reason enough to shuffle over
to the medical tent on a fact-finding mission.

Rumor became substantiated fact in cold black-and-white:

> 9:30 A.M. weather forecast for 5/13/92
> Rap song of the day . . .
> Second storm same as the first,
> a little more windy and somewhat worse!
> Due to arrive later.
> Enjoy today's window.
> (We're not in Kansas anymore, Toto . . .)

Cute! Our fate was reduced to two lines and a rap jingle.
At least the ranger had a sense of humor. . . . Guess you would
have to, being stationed up here by choice.

As for the "weather window," it wasn't much to be enjoyed.
The wind and snow continued to swirl.

I ran into Wickwire on the way back to the tent. According
to him, at an overnight low of minus-27 degrees Fahrenheit and

winds in excess of 100 miles per hour, this weather rated as the coldest he'd ever seen on the mountain—this from a man who'd scaled Denali three times, once in February.

Craig failed to lift my spirits by resorting to rough calculations when I returned to the tent. Factoring in the wind chill, the temperature had plunged to well below minus-150 degrees Fahrenheit. My little slice of the world began to feel very much colder than before.

Robert's head poked into the tent. "How are you all doing? This next storm coming in has forced our hand. We've got to go down now and collect our remaining supplies, and we've got to do it fast." The urgency in his voice was obvious. Without food and fuel, our situation could go from bad to deadly in a matter of moments. Our lives depended on getting to that cache and back up here before the next storm hit and without falling into the many crevasses lurking in our path. Worse, our cache was situated right below a potential avalanche chute made even more dangerous with all the new snow.

Desperate for some activity to help me keep warm and prevent my mind from drifting in morbid directions, I volunteered to go. Craig, still feeling the effects of yesterday's overexertion, stayed behind to watch the camp. We got down to the cache without incident but once there, Robert exploded like a volcano.

"Shit! Some asshole has broken into our cache and ransacked our food supply. . . . Some of it's gone. I'm gonna kick some . . . !" His voice trailed off as he stormed around the pit, punching one hand into the other.

The gravity and weight of what had happened settled down on us like a suffocating cloak of iron. Every good mountaineer has a contingency just-in-case plan, such as a few days of extra food, perhaps some extra fuel. Very often, it can mean the difference between life and death. With a portion of our food now stolen, however, our contingency supplies and plans were no more. If the unthinkable were to happen, the person or persons who stole our food would be responsible for our deaths, plain and simple. This was a violation of mountaineering ethics, of the worst kind. An act akin to stealing a cowboy's horse in the Wild West, leaving him to walk or die under a desert sun—an action that warranted hanging or shooting.

There was nothing left to do but gather up what food and supplies remained and pack them up to camp. Our lives now depended on our ability to stretch the food supplies, which meant reducing vital caloric intake and leaving ourselves more vulnerable to whatever the mountain presented. Still, as long as we could stay warm, dry, protected, and well hydrated, we would be okay for the time being.

That evening, in the snow cave during dinner, the radio crackled with the voices of the Koreans above us. Apparently they had made it to 15,000 feet, but they were panicking. Through all the static and problems caused by the language barrier, we managed to understand that they wanted a rescue helicopter. It didn't take much imagination to guess at what was going on. The Koreans were freezing to death on the mountain and all anyone could do was listen. The mountain was beginning to exact payment from those who dared not listen to its words of warning—first the Italians, now the Koreans.

As I lay in my sleeping bag that night, struggling to stay warm, my thoughts drifted to Jan, one of my oldest and best friends who had died a few months before this climb. We both harbored a passion for the mountains. If it hadn't been for a lifetime of illness, she would have shared these experiences with me. Calling her hospital daily, I asked the attending nurse to hold the phone to my friend's ear. I remained undaunted by the one-sided nature of our communication. When the new occupant of Jan's hospital bed answered my final call, the realization of her passing chilled me. Ours was a difficult parting of ways.

I had a feeling that, here on Denali, she was now closer to me than she had been in life. For all I knew, it was she who was acting as my guardian. I had dedicated this climb to her memory with the idea of making the attempt a celebration of her life and the mountain a monument to her achievements. Now, huddled in my personal icebox, I wondered if my experience would become more a struggle for survival than a celebration of life.

THURSDAY, MAY 14
Day twelve on the mountain

"It's not looking good, Craig." My morning opener was taking on all the trappings of cliché.

"Tell me something new . . . please," Craig implored.

Trouble was, there was nothing new to tell, except that the wind was now howling through camp at 120 miles per hour like an out-of-control beast with devilish intentions. It tore across ridges, ripped through crevasses, snatched at anything not securely fastened, and vibrated the ground to which we clung for our lives. I awoke truly grateful for small things such as the relative warmth of my sleeping bag and the fact that our tent still stood in one piece, though for how much longer was anyone's guess.

The pain my partially thawed feet were experiencing was a mixed blessing. As long as I could feel pain, I knew my feet were relatively okay and not frozen solid. On the other hand, the pain was too intense to sleep through, leaving me no alternative but to lie awake for hours on end and contemplate our fate.

Craig and I ventured beyond our tent walls only to take a dump and to crawl to the snow cave for breakfast and dinner. Simply heading for a meal proved to be an arduous adventure. Paul burst into the cave at one point, his face twisted with fear and his eyes as big as plates. "Ohmigod . . . I just got knocked off my feet . . . driven across the ground like a dust particle."

There was no reason to step outside to check the weather. From inside our battered tents, it became obvious that we were becoming part of history—the worst storm on record. Even the ranger stayed in his tent, no longer posting weather signs on the medical station. Probably a good thing since the situation had become too grim to put in writing. No news, in this case, was undoubtedly better than the truth.

Our team hunkered down, encapsulated in orange tents only a few feet apart. Despite the physical closeness, we huddled in an insular world beyond sight and sound of one another. Even during our brief meals together, the two times we came together as a team, a thin veneer of isolation prevailed. No one said much. Conversation would only distract from the primary mission—

eat fast before your meal or your feet froze. Win's feet had become frostbitten the night before while cooking in our spacious cavern.

Today, at breakfast, the mood was sullen. Robert had been to Denali seven times previously and had never seen temperatures so cold—which made the rest of us feel even colder. Here we sat, waiting like little Oliver Twists for a portion of breakfast gruel, contemplating the significance of being trapped in the epicenter of cold and violence.

"I wonder what it feels like to actually be warm," mused Randy to no one in particular. "I mean, do you realize that when I get home, I will be 240 degrees warmer than I am now? Unless they heat things up around here, Denali is going to the bottom of my destination resorts list."

Randy's words and attempt at humor fell heavily to the floor, which is where I felt like tossing breakfast. Eating was a chore, an activity tolerated only because our bodies needed food to stay warm and strong. At a calculated 150 degrees below zero with the wind chill, you will put up with anything that resembles food—regardless of taste and appearance.

"If it makes you feel any better, I gave this climb to myself as a birthday present," I responded in an attempt to console him.

Randy looked up from his bowl, gave me a thin smile and mumbled, "Happy birthday." End of conversation. End of breakfast.

Back inside our tent, Craig and I took a physical inventory motivated by hearing about a climber from another camp who, after digging out his tent, took a sip of hot tea and cracked all his teeth. Just like that, with no warning. One minute he was very cold and the next he was very cold with broken teeth. If the mountain could exact such misery from the hardest part of the human body, what did that say about the vulnerability of flesh? We began to suspect that our body parts might soon begin to break off from the cold—a grimly humorous notion.

It didn't take much scrutiny to reveal my condition. My face looked like dog meat. I was grateful my husband wasn't there to see me like that. My cracked lips bled constantly. Frostbite had left crusty scabs on my nose and cheeks. Besides my toes, my thumbs were beginning to turn black as well. My thumbs fascinated me. Despite wrapping the head of my ice ax in foam to protect my hands from the frozen metal, my thumbs, which rested slightly against the metal shaft when I was using the ax had been frostbitten—even through heavy down expedition mitts. Craig and I shared a rather perverse fascination staring at each other's damaged parts and at ourselves using the tiny mirror I had packed. The image of my reflected appearance was disturbing. As I stared at the bleeding face with sunken eyes and drawn cheeks I retreated deeply into my soul searching for answers to questions no one dared pose.

"Aging—good thing it mellows the soul because it sure does shit for the body," I murmured into the air, fingering my battered flesh.

Craig rolled over and stared. "A few more days of this crap and we won't have to worry about growing old, we'll be there already."

One doctor I knew had labeled me a "medical anomaly." In second grade, the misdiagnosis of a heart condition confined me to bed for a year with the prognosis of a life condemned to a wheelchair. After accepting my fate with passive resignation as only a child can, a Mayo Clinic exam uncovered the mistake. My new lease on life became a treasure never taken for granted.

In my mid-thirties, despite a healthy lifestyle, physical problems besieged me once more. Four major surgeries in as many years inspired the neighborhood children to call me the bionic woman. A chronic virus that stripped my immune system had compounded the difficulties and prompted my husband Bob to wonder if I had come with a warranty.

I turned to the mountains for healing, scheduling a climb on Kilimanjaro three months after my final surgery, dubbed the "human head transplant"—a procedure to align my jaw that took two surgeons four hours to complete. Needing a medical release signed before I made the journey, I paid a visit to my family doctor.

"You know, Ruth Anne, if it were anyone else but you, I wouldn't sign this."

"And if you don't, you know I will," I shot back.

A mountaineer himself, he dispensed with the formalities and laughed. He signed the form, wishing he was going, too.

A few years later, while on Rainier, I ruptured a disk under the weight of a heavy pack and then further aggravated it stepping out of a helicopter while powder skiing in Canada. The attending doctor's doom-and-gloom admonition to never run or climb again annoyed me, but it was the twenty-three-year-old physical therapist who pushed me to anger.

"Face it, you're forty-one," she lectured. "Why don't you just accept that?"

"Why don't I just lie down and die!" I blasted back at her.

Ever the mistress of denial, and far from my death bed, I summited Aconcagua nine months later. Now, here I lay on Denali with a back that was aching from prolonged inactivity and the tricky maneuvers required to dress inside a restricted four-by-five-foot tent space. I still had too much life in me to just lie down and die. Right then and there I made up my mind: I was going to summit this mountain.

"What day is today?" Craig's question snapped me back to the present.

"Thursday."

He thought for a minute and then made a face. "Who really cares . . . what difference does it make, anyway? All it really means is that yesterday was Wednesday." With that, he threw himself back down onto his frozen pillow, covered his eyes with his arm, and moaned.

Oh God! He was at it again, computing the duration of our stay on Denali given every possible turn of events. This routine of counting and calculating the days and hours in his mind would drive him (and me) crazy. Waiting is the hardest part of mountaineering. If we were to maintain our sanity and health we had to let go of time and not fight it. The weather would pass, but on its own schedule, not ours.

Remaining patient under extreme stress is not easy, however. Teams were running out of supplies and leaving our 14,000-foot encampment in a headlong rush to get off the mountain. That night at dinner in the dining cave, Paul seemed anxious and finally blurted out, "Look, that German team came by today and said they're leaving because they think tomorrow will be too late! And I talked to the leader of the international team. They're leaving as soon as the weather breaks enough because he said he can't be responsible for killing anyone."

The specter of doubt about our own position raised the question in all of our minds about our own decision to stay put. Who was making the right decision—us or them? We looked at Robert.

"People are literally dying to get off this mountain," Robert observed grimly, and with that terse commentary, the discussion was over.

Retreating posed as great a danger as going up, and certainly more than staying put.

Rationing our resources allowed us the luxury of patience and eliminated the perception that we should take unnecessary risks. We had calculated, considering our remaining food supplies and fuel situation, that we could stretch our mountain stay to ten more days. That meant that, if the weather lifted early next week as rumored, we would have just enough provisions to see us to the peak and back down again safely. For now, there was security and wisdom in staying put.

But staying put also forced us to ride an emotional roller coaster. We had come to climb but instead found ourselves trapped in a tiny corner of the planet just eating, sleeping, sitting, shitting, shoveling, urinating, talking, and ruminating. We had no immediate purpose other than to survive another minute, another hour, as the hours turned to days. Wild mood swings were common—one minute hopeful, the next depressed.

Our sleeping bags now served a double purpose. The struggle to maintain sanity in the face of this high-intensity tedium was taking its toll. Concerned that we might be driven to bizarre behavior, violence even, our sleeping bags doubled as zippered straitjackets, protecting us from ourselves. Until this climb, my notion of hell on earth had been the waiting room of a doctor's office with the schedule running far behind. The minutes were etched into our minds with the violence of the wind and the monotony of the tent. Craig began to joke that we were going to get bedsores from lying around so much.

Suddenly, Craig wriggled out of his sleeping bag and began throwing on his gear.

"Oh, dammit," Craig moaned. "I can't hold it any longer. I've gotta go outside."

I felt for him. During my last trip outside to shovel off the tent, the force of the wind caused my eyes to water profusely, even with goggles on, and the cold froze my tears to my face and in my eyes. The scene in front of me had clouded instantly as though I was peering through waxed paper. Blinking didn't help, either, since my eyelids then froze shut.

Craig's destination was the community latrine—the mountain commode. In calmer weather, the view from atop the wooden throne was memorable, as was everyone else's view of you—bare ass to the wind. Today, anyone on the throne was bare-ass to the cold, turning an ordinary human function into a mind-bending ordeal of pushing and praying. Frostbite on the buttocks and, for the males, on other parts of the anatomy, was not out of the question if one's business was not concluded quickly.

"Oh my God!" Craig burst back into the tent wild-eyed and breathing heavily. He'd crawled only as far as the perimeter of our ice-block wall surrounding the tent. "That's it! If things get any worse, I'm gonna find me a cork, pound it into my ass, and not pull it out until we get off this damn mountain."

Freezing your ass off had suddenly taken on an entirely new and not-so-humorous meaning. I knew how he felt because, since yesterday, I had resorted to something that I would never have considered, a pee bottle when I needed to urinate. Issues of modesty were taking a backseat to the only real issue that mattered— survival.

Urinating indoors and into a bottle wasn't all that bad. For guys, it's easy, just point and shoot. For me, the technique required a little more effort, but it beat the hell out of going outdoors. The key was in creating a tight seal between the bottle and me because there was no way I wanted to miss and wet my clothes or sleeping bag. The biggest problem with the pee bottle was freezing. A bottle was good for about two uses before it required emptying, but in most cases, the urine would freeze before I could empty it. That meant standing around outdoors beating on the bottle to break up the ice before dumping it out or tucking it in next to me in the sleeping bag to thaw it so I could empty it.

Since the pee bottle was really just a wide-mouth water bottle, the same size and shape as the water bottle I drank out of, I had to be extra careful when I went for a drink. I could imagine nothing worse than slaking my thirst on the wrong bottle.

A deck of cards appeared almost miraculously in Craig's hands. He had been rummaging around his gear since burrowing into his sleeping bag.

"Want to play a hand or two?"

Like I had something better to do. "Sure, what game?" As

if I couldn't have guessed. There is only one game that two people can play for hours at a time while confined in a tent: gin rummy. I had never been so grateful for something as simple as a deck of cards. In a search for salvation from the monotony and cold, the gin rummy marathon was born.

We took frequent breaks to rewarm our hands or unglue the cards that kept freezing together in the extreme cold. Despite the adversity, we played hand after hand. Craig struggled to write the scores in the back of his journal, but that, too, was made nearly impossible with the cold. He really didn't need to bother. It wasn't the scores that mattered, only playing. Actually, we were playing two games—one with cards and the other with our minds as we struggled to block out the violence surrounding our tent.

The wind continued to barrel down the mountain walls around us like an out-of-control locomotive. A distant rumbling heralded the approach of each onslaught moments before a blast slammed into camp. And, with each blast, our tent would strain against the wind as the storm sought to rip it from the block of ice to which it was moored. Each time the tent lifted and shook we clung tightly to it and our cards, wondering whether or not this was the moment when the nylon shroud would take us for a ride. My stomach muscles ached from the effort required to brace for each pummeling. At times, we weren't sure whether we were safer inside or out. If I could have made myself heavier, I would have.

As far-fetched as it may seem, being blown off the mountain wasn't out of the realm of possibility, and had nearly happened to Robert during a summit attempt on Everest. He and Pete

Whittaker were camped at 27,000 feet when they felt their tent begin to move from under them in the high winds. Grabbing boots, parkas, and other pieces of essential gear, they managed to get out just as their shelter was plucked off the mountainside and hurled into the black of night. Eleven of fourteen tents suffered the same fate that night. Craig didn't appreciate the story.

"Gin!" Thank God for the game and for Craig who kept yelling, "Gin!" at all the right moments when the tension needed to be broken. His years between emergency calls had made him a deadly gamesman with a deck of cards, and I was his captive victim—he was killing me. But I could have kept on losing forever. We finally had something to do. In winning, Craig was finding a sliver of control in an otherwise uncontrollable situation.

{6} ROARING DREAMS TAKE PLACE IN SILENT MINDS

———✦———

FRIDAY, MAY 15
Day thirteen on the mountain

T he roar of the storm pried its way past my earplugs, jolting my body out of its state of restless slumber. Before consciousness swept the fog of sleep from my mind, I found myself dreaming a distant dream of a tiny boat being dashed about in a violent sea with the sails ripped to shreds and slapping wildly against the mast and hull.

As I awoke, my feet, still frozen, began to throb painfully—an excruciating, burning sensation that knifed up my legs and spread through my body like thousands of red-hot needles being thrust into my skin. The pain was inescapable, one that made me writhe and want to scream. The bright side to the pain, though, was that it indicated my feet were getting warmer, and better, despite the numbing temperatures all around.

I slept with everything I owned either worn or piled on top of me—down bag, down parka, down vest, fleece pants, expedition-weight long underwear—everything, and still I was barely, just barely, warm enough. The temperature had plummeted to minus-45 degrees Fahrenheit overnight. Visibility dropped to zero. A colorless diabolical world filled with deafening noise besieged us from every direction. Everything moved—

the wind, the tents, the ground—but mostly the snow. Snow lay all over the inside of the tent. Despite our best efforts to keep the weather outside, each time the tent door opened, more snow blew in. We returned to the tent with pounds of snow clinging to our clothing every time we ventured outside, if only for a moment or two. The snow never seemed to melt, yet somehow everything in the tent managed to get damp and then frozen solid. We were our only source of heat so that if anything needed to be thawed, it went into our sleeping bags in the hopes that our body heat could warm it before it chilled us to the bone. As if conditions weren't bad enough, frost cascaded down from the ceiling of the tent constantly, jarred loose by the snapping and popping of the tent fabric shaking before the impacts of endless explosions. We were embroiled in the glacial version of Dante's *Inferno*.

I became conscious of the fact that, lying there in my sleeping bag, I was damp and becoming increasingly chilled.

"Craig?"

"Mmm, yeah?" He was half asleep. Sleep was one of the few defenses in a losing battle with the boredom and inactivity we faced.

"I've got to get out of this wet stuff 'cause I'm freezing, and I'm sorry."

"Say what? What are you sorry for?" Craig seemed concerned that I might be losing it.

"I'm sorry that when I leap out of this bag and begin tearing off my clothes I'm going to destroy whatever fantasy you may yet cling to regarding the pleasure of gazing at a woman's body."

Craig smiled, obviously relieved that I was making an attempt at humor and not really losing it.

"Thanks for the warning. I'd hate to have the one fantasy that's keeping me going shattered forever." And with that he did the wise thing and rolled over.

Even inside the tent, I could feel the force of the wind cutting through the seams, pushing its way through the tent's zippers. The swirling arctic air inside, accompanied by the shock-wave explosions of the storm knocking at the tent trying to get in, took my breath away. I rushed back into my sleeping bag to regain precious body heat. My world extended only as far as the sides of my mummy bag, a term that had taken on new meaning as we clung to our icy perch on the very brink of extinction. Here in our fabric crypt, the baseline for misery was hitting a new low.

Being confined to spaces smaller than myself had been the story of my life. By eighth grade, my body had stretched to five-feet-nine inches, while tipping the scales at a scant 100 pounds. I had to bend over to get into my locker, scrunch down to sit at my desk. My waiflike physique impressed others, but for all the wrong reasons. With my white-blonde hair, I couldn't very well hide, though Lord knows I wanted to.

"My goodness dear . . . you have grown, haven't you!" friends of my parents and other adults would routinely exclaim.

My face and neck would then turn a bright shade of red as I mumbled through the obligatory, "Yeah, well, I guess," while the adults just stared, making little attempt to hide their personal amazement. Applying the Chinese practice of binding the feet to binding my body in a modified way would have won my vote. Only a mother could refer to such a gawky form as a "model's figure." She continually assured me that I was merely a late bloomer and that I would soon grow into my body and learn to appreciate my physical assets ... eventually. The task of growing so consumed me that I harbored no illusions of a life filled with athletics. Keeping up with my own body posed enough of a physical challenge. Though active, I never won so much as a last place ribbon in any sporting event. Early in high school, my lack of coordination drove me to the swimming pool just so I could get off my feet. Emerging from the water two years later, I discovered that not only could I walk, but my body and coordination were actually now talking to each other—in fact, I became quite athletically adept.

To my great relief the endless vertical process finally ceased, leaving me a towering six feet by the end of high school and the tallest girl of a class of twelve hundred. My friends labeled me "Whitey Stilts." When I walked down the aisle last during graduation ceremonies, I was consoled slightly by the fact that at least some of the boys had begun to grow, too.

"What are you smiling at now?" Craig was once again gazing intently my way.

"Can't you sleep?"

"Are you kidding? All we've been doing is sleeping, eating, and shitting. I'm too bored to sleep, and shitting for entertainment lost its appeal a long time ago. Eating ... well, if we had more food I'd be eating myself silly, but we don't so ... Why are you smiling?"

"I was just thinking back to my childhood and the nickname

my friends used to put on me—'Whitey Stilts.' Can you imagine that?"

"I can imagine just about anything right now. . . . Okay, so entertain me. Tell me a story from your childhood and make it a good one. . . . I want off this damn mountain for a while."

I understood Craig's need all too well. We were all going crazy, sitting or lying around, or, weather permitting, milling about in the storm like cattle, simply searching for something to do, anything. A couple of guys from Jackson Hole fought off boredom by building an elaborately engineered ice-block wall around the latrine for privacy—spent several hours cutting, stacking, shaping. It was a nice effort, but didn't last long. The first to test the newly sheltered throne found himself momentarily buried under an avalanche of ice blocks and snow as the wind ripped the wall apart. Better him than me, I remembered thinking while at the same time wondering if we shouldn't try to rebuild the wall—just for something to do.

And so I launched into a story that was as much for my benefit as for his. You see, boredom never has brought out the best in me. As the oldest child in a large family my parents drilled me to set a good example. In their presence, I managed to maintain the charade, but inside a monster waited and paced, yearning to be released. In school, a lack of challenge motivated me to create my own adventures. As the instigator of pranks, I routinely slipped away unscathed while others took the blame. Fortunately, I had the good sense to stay out of serious trouble other than that one little felony. . . .

Early in high school I broke into a deserted home, never expecting reality to exceed my imagination and actually produce a treasure. The myth that Old Joe, a recluse armed with a shot-gun, lurked in the overgrown, neglected, and abandoned ruin had prevented anyone from attempting to explore the building. The neighborhood eyesore remained boarded up for thirty years until, one rainy day, curiosity overcame any latent fear and con-vinced me to investigate.

After fighting through a heap of bedsprings, rocking chairs, and orange crates, I finally managed to reach the entry. When I tried the front door, the latch fell out of the rotting wood, and the door swung open, slowly. The combination of the squeaking hinges in desperate need of oil, the darkness beyond the thresh-old, and the sudden surge of fetid air that now enveloped me, convinced me of the wisdom in enlisting a companion.

It didn't take long for me to find a friend who shared my curiosity for this old place. We returned to the house and boldly strode through the front door. In the rush to grab supplies suit-able for our covert operation, we failed to locate flashlights and opted for readily accessible candles. The odor of mildew, dust, and decomposing wood rendered the blackness suffocating. The flickering flames of our two tiny candles emitted a dancing light that cast an eerie, wavering glow that, while deceiving to our eyes, illuminated quite clearly the fact that we stood inside a veritable fire trap.

To mask our uneasiness, we spoke loudly while taking un-usual interest in the wide variety of objects around us. A cast-iron stove sat in the corner while rodent-infested boxes of Wheaties featuring Babe Ruth on the front panel littered the floor. A dust-covered bottle of whiskey stood half-empty atop a china cabinet and an overcoat draped a chair nearby. Above the wall phone, bearing a note to *"pick up eggs,"* hung a picture of the house in its earlier years. Stacks of newspapers five feet tall filled the room, so much that only a narrow path led between them.

My friend forged ahead, working her way deeper and deeper into the house while I, fearing the worst, feigned great interest in the stacks of periodicals. Headlines such as "War Declared," "Nazis Hit Front," and "Pearl Harbor Bombed," screamed out that we had indeed stepped through the door and back into time. Not wanting to be left alone, I followed my friend, all the while reconfirming the escape route over my shoulder.

We made our way through veils of cobwebs, passing two antiquated bikes, their balloon tires long since turned to dust. An array of unopened Christmas gifts lay scattered about, containing vestiges of the past, from wide, floral-print ties to single-slot toasters. I marveled at the unused appliances that predated my friend's and my lifetime, still in their original packaging. It was the unopened letters written in German, however, that piqued my curiosity to a fiery level. The postmarks from the thirties convinced us that we were on to a big mystery and we might just find the answers deeper inside.

The realization that we were moving farther into a structurally unsafe building did not escape me. A single two-by-four wedged between the floor and the ceiling at an odd angle supported the entire sagging structure. Alarm turned to horror when I discovered that the same makeshift post was precariously balanced on a stack of books. To this point, I had worried only about our candles starting a fire amid all the trash and burning us to death. Now, however, I discovered the near-paralyzing fear of being crushed to death if the entire place tumbled down around us.

Getting out took on a renewed urgency, especially with our lungs choked by the layers of dust stirred by the first feet to wander within this house in decades. We turned quickly to leave and in so doing, knocked into a mound of newspapers, toppling them to the floor and revealing yet another unopened door behind them. Curiosity overruled fear once again. While clearing away the debris, my eyes seized on the plaster hand of a mannequin, gray from age and dust. The absence of an adjoining body seemed strangely in keeping with our discoveries within this house of mystery.

An evil thought crept into my brain. My friend never noticed me strategically placing the body part among the piles of paper. On spotting the hand sticking out of the paper and grasping at air, she became so viscerally affected that her bladder let loose, leaving her standing in a puddle. Her bold veneer thus cracked, I took over the lead, foraging farther into the bowels of the house.

Behind the door, a narrow, winding staircase led up to the second floor. Ignoring the two-by-four prop that would hopefully hold up the floor below us, we made our way up. Our nerves certainly didn't gain a boost in confidence when the door slammed shut behind us. Several strange creaks and bangs later, we crept into one of the two bedrooms. A dusty brass bed stood on one side, the yellowed sheets pulled back as though someone had just slept there. On the cover lay a jacket, pants, and a pair of high-button dress shoes. Small articles from a man's pocket lay strewn across a table—change, bus tokens, Chicago World's

Fair trinkets, hexagonal-shaped spectacles, and Beechnut gum in brown paper wrappers.

Lured on by the intriguing trail of objects, we skirted the pronounced dip in the floor while entertaining visions of discovering the missing body belonging to the hand below. We opened store boxes of unworn clothes and discovered a Tiffany lamp under the bed. A yellowed envelope, containing a perfect five-dollar gold piece, fell from between the pages of a leather-bound Bible. We rifled through drawers and discovered items of another era—spats, collars, and cuffs. As my eyes settled on a revolver and a box of bullets tucked under some shirts, my friend let out a muffled cry. With my heart leaping from my chest, I spun, coming face-to-face with a handful of money thrust into my face. Clutched in her hands was a stack of green bills, wrapped in bank notes: $850 by our count. A wave of nausea swept over me as my first impulse was to drop the money and run, run until we had escaped the house, until we escaped the reality of the gun and money. We had gone too far. My friend argued that we had to take the money now that we had found it, that it could no longer be safely left in place. Her logic won over my emotions and we smuggled the contraband out of the house and to her home.

We spent the afternoon arguing. I was adamant that the money should never have been touched. My friend was equally adamant that we had no choice. After weighing the consequences of trespassing, breaking and entering, and now, robbery, we resigned to turn ourselves in. Dealing with the law seemed a far preferable option to having to deal with our parents. Although my friend wanted to dress in disguise as an old woman and claim her daughter had stumbled on the loot, I had reached my imagination's limit. We would go to the authorities immediately before the situation became more convoluted.

On the way to the police station, we rehearsed our story repeatedly, walking and talking, talking and walking. The officer on duty listened attentively as we detailed our crime. Suddenly he interrupted.

"I can't believe you girls are turning in all this money. I sure wouldn't have!"

Confusion reigned supreme. My friend glared at me and I just shrugged my shoulders. I couldn't have dealt with the guilt anyway. The officer told us that Old Joe had lived alone in the house until abruptly being declared incompetent and carted off to an institution. His home remained tied up in the estate. The officer assured us that he would personally deliver the money to the relatives. Instincts told me he wouldn't.

Having been spared the legal consequences of our actions, we felt cautiously secure in recounting the extraordinary tale to our parents. Uncertain as to whether their response would border on punishment or accolades, we approached each of our parents in tandem. There was, after all, safety in numbers. Their reactions ranged from disbelief, coupled with a show of disgust, to wonder. Although compelled to reprimand us, they found the escapade captivating. During a moment of weakness my own mother lamented our failure to abscond with the Tiffany lamp before turning ourselves in.

Several weeks passed before I noticed the front door of the abandoned house ajar and the wooden panels torn from the windows. Peeking in the door, I could see clearly that the place had been stripped of its contents. All that remained were hundreds of bank bands littering the floor.

It took a few years but I gradually came to understand adventure as a challenge rather than an event inspired by a sense of mischief and reckless abandon.

"I'd have turned the money in, too." Craig was lying on his back, staring at the ceiling. "All those bank bands, though. . . . You guys must have discovered just the tip of the treasure haul. Wow! Unbelievable."

We slept some more. And then we headed to dinner, making the second of our twice-a-day trips to the ice cooler we called the kitchen. The entrance had been reduced to a small hole in the snow, forcing us to lie down and slide in facefirst to enter and crawl out combat-style on our bellies to exit. During our brief time each day in the cave, we shared light conversation. It was getting increasingly difficult to remain upbeat.

Robert announced that, since we were running low on fuel, we would no longer be using the stoves to melt snow for water. This meant each of us would have to sleep with our water bottles to thaw them out and then carry them around with us inside our parkas all day, like babies. Just as long as one of them didn't decide to take a leak on me, I could handle it.

No one cared much about getting to the top anymore. As bad as retorts were, none of us was getting enough to eat. Without adequate food in our bodies, it was almost impossible to keep the energy level up. Win reported that even if we conserved our twenty-one-day supply of food, we'd likely consume all of it *before* we managed to get off the mountain.

"As long as we stay dry, warm, protected, and reasonably hydrated, there is no reason to believe we will not make the summit or that there will be any problems," said Win, trying to put a positive spin on things.

We all knew what he meant, though. No problems for the short run—but what if the storm kept up its relentless assault? What then? We were holding together ... barely.

"Look, I want to go up, if the weather allows us, and I just know we can make it if we stick together on this." Franklin was gazing around the cave, trying to catch each person's stare. "I had to turn back from this same elevation last year because of pulmonary edema, but this year I feel great. Dammit, I'm not going to let this mountain get away from me a second time!"

"I'd like to get to the top, too, but my priorities have shifted to getting off of this mountain safely," John offered. Craig and I nodded in agreement.

"Well, I'm expected back at my office on Tuesday so ... well, I really do need to get back soon, you know." Vern was a piece of work, of that there could be no argument.

"I think you're going to have to call in," fired back Randy, rolling his eyes in disgust. "We'll wait here while you go find a phone."

"Look, I am sure the weather will break early next week and getting down from the mountain safely is not going to be the issue—only going up—and if the weather remains the same, we won't *be* going up," added Win.

"Win's right." Robert chimed in quietly but firmly. "This storm will likely suck in a big high-pressure ridge which would give us the four-day window to the summit we need. We're going to wait it out and hope for the break we need by early next week, okay?"

We all nodded in agreement and then crawled off in the direction of our tents.

The urge to pee hit me around the middle of the night, squeezing my bladder until I could take it no longer. Realizing I hadn't emptied my pee bottle, I was forced to either hold fast or head outside to dump and purge. Cursing, I dressed quickly, grabbed the full bottle, and plunged into the swirling ice milk on my hands and knees. Within seconds, I completely lost sight of our tent. Thinking my goggles were the problem, I lifted them to get a better view and my eyes froze shut. Perfect. Somehow, my mental map of the landscape held true and I managed to reverse my direction and crawl the few feet back to our tent and dive indoors to thaw.

"Goddamn!"

Craig stirred and looked up. "Problem?"

"Yeah, you could say that. My eyes just froze shut and I had to crawl back in here blind."

"No shit? Damn, woman. You be careful out there."

"No worries. I thought that the reason I couldn't see the tent after I crawled away from it was that my goggles had fogged or frozen up. Turns out the reason I couldn't see is that it's snowing so damn hard—still. I've got to go back out, though, and dump this bottle and pee before I explode."

With my eyes thawed and my goggles back in place, I dove

back into the maelstrom. Even with the goggles on, my eyes began to tear and the tears began to freeze, making my vision blurry, not that I could see much of anything anyway. Mountaineering by Braille—not one of my top ten favorite adventure choices, mind you. Fortunately, I didn't need to see to pee. I'd remember to dump my bottle during the day in future, that's for sure. My business done, I scurried back to the tent and wriggled deeply into the relative warmth of my sleeping bag.

SATURDAY. MAY 16
Day fourteen on the mountain

It felt colder this morning and, to make matters worse, the weight of the snow piling up around the outside of our tent was beginning to squeeze us inward. There was definitely no sign of an impending warming trend or weather window. I glanced over at Craig who was performing his perfunctory finger-count analysis of our situation.

"One, two, three, four, five, six . . . Shit!. We've been stuck here at 14,000 feet for six days!" Craig was gazing at his four upthrust fingers and thumb on one hand and index finger on the other as if questioning what they were telling him. "Six days. Oh Lord! . . . We were supposed to be on the summit today, weren't we?"

"Uh-huh, but no use in worrying about that now," I tried to offer soothingly, although in my state, I'm not sure I managed very well. It's hard to sound soothing when your voice is cracking and your nerves are on edge from living within ground zero of a weather explosion.

If we were lucky and the weather actually lifted, we'd probably begin doing carries to 16,500 feet Monday or Tuesday. That would leave us moving to high camp at 17,200 feet to spend the night and, hopefully, to summit the next day.

With our claustrophobia mounting and having exhausted any interest I might have had for gin rummy, my thoughts turned to the three books we had among the ten of us in order to save my sanity—*The Firm, The Icarus Agenda,* and a book on fighter planes.

"I've got to find one of those books I know we brought along or I think I'm going to lose my mind," I told Craig as I pulled on my layers of clothing and proceeded to duck out into the storm. "Want anything?"

"Nah. I'll just read whatever you bring back once you're done.... Happy hunting."

I secured *The Firm* from Robert and spent a few minutes engaged in storm talk before heading back to my tent. *The Icarus Agenda* sounded good, too, but a bit heavy for my tastes. As for the book on fighter planes, I'd pass, even if it were the last book on earth—nothing could possibly be so bad I'd read a book like that.

While spending a few minutes furiously digging out the tent, I saw it. Actually, Paul saw it first and pointed it out.

"Hey, Ruth Anne—check it out. Whaddaya think's up with that?"

I looked over and saw a sleeping bag being dragged across

camp on a sled toward the medical tent. Looking back at Paul, I shrugged my shoulders. It was a peculiar vision to say the least. Paul strolled over beside me and we both watched them drag the bag.

"Man, that guy must *really* be sick, you think? I mean, something bad like hypothermia or something."

"I have no idea Paul, but it can't be good, whatever it is." I could feel the muscles in my stomach begin to tighten, my breath begin to shorten.

We stood and watched as the ranger dragged a large red bag from the storage tent next to the medical tent. Quickly, the sleeping bag and its heavy contents were hoisted from the sled and deposited unceremoniously into the bag, which was then zipped shut. Moving from one end of the bag to the other, the ranger tightened draw straps to secure the cargo—one end across the chest and the other around the ankles. With the tightening of straps, the bag now conformed to the body, giving it the look of a plastic-coated mummy. The body was clearly resting on its back. Two others, probably team members of the fallen one, dragged the body bag to the side of the storage tent, marked either end with ski poles (so they could find it when it came time to dig out), and then walked away. That was it—no service, no memorial. Just zip and dump.

It just lay there, faceup and "looking" toward Mount Foraker. There was no way for anyone to fly in and pick up the body and it was too dangerous to attempt to drag it down the mountain. So, the body was simply parked here, tangible proof that death had moved beyond the rumor stage and was now camped at 14,000 feet with us.

"Ruth Anne?" Paul called out with a hollow voice as he stared at the body bag.

"Yeah?"

"Ruth Anne, it just occurred to me that I could really get hurt up here, couldn't I?" His voice quavered a bit, either from nerves or tears—with the goggles on, it was hard to tell.

I just nodded in agreement, although inside, I had an almost uncontrollable urge to grab him by the jacket collar and scream, "Just occurred to you? *JUST* OCCURRED TO YOU? Where the hell have you been!?"

I needed to know more, so I wandered stiffly over to the ranger's tent through the raging storm. I didn't find out much, other than his name—Alex Von Bergen—and age—forty-two. According to Paul, who had spoken briefly with him the day before, Alex was a very experienced Swiss guide. I knew that his tent sat only yards from ours. I also knew from Paul that Alex had seemed very healthy. The ranger had mentioned that although the cause of death was uncertain, he suspected a massive edema and pulmonary complications. His body had simply failed and that was what was so frightening.

Not ready to go back to the confines of my sleeping bag just yet, and needing to rejuvenate my prosthetic feet, I shuffled over to the body bag and stood at its feet. My own vulnerability, our entire team's vulnerability, came crashing down on me like a tsunami wave. My knees began to sag under the force of emotional impact. It bothered me knowing that every time I stepped out of my tent, the body would be just over there, staring up into space, reminding me of life's frailty.

It was that he was alone here—more than his being dead—

that began to get to me most, though. I stood there and wondered, Why you and not me, why not all of us? I'd always assumed until now that there was a baseline for human survival. Now I wasn't so sure. I wanted to ask him what his expectations had been for this climb, what his plans were afterward. Whatever they might have been, they were over. To be frozen there in the storm seemed to me an interruption of the process. Alex was dead and now it was time to move on—both for him and for us. Somehow it didn't seem fair to have him held hostage in limbo rather than allowing him to depart to whatever was supposed to come next. It seemed like such an alone place to be—stuck here with the living . . . together . . . in the storm . . . in time.

I had stood vigil by a body once before, not by choice, during an incident in my early teens while working as a lifeguard. Two hundred children filled a pool when a commotion broke loose in the shallow end. Two boys clung rigidly to the side of the pool as electricity from a shorted underwater light passed through them. A radius of current coursed through the water, preventing others from advancing closer to attempt a rescue.

I watched the coach run over. He reached down and was promptly hurled off his feet and backward by the shock. Never giving up, he repeated his efforts until he somehow managed to drag both of them onto the pool deck, and an all-out resuscitation effort began. In the meantime, the other lifeguards, including me, evacuated scores of youngsters still in the pool and very much at risk.

Forty-five minutes passed in a flash as we ushered all the children from the pool to the deck and into the safety of the locker rooms. As quickly as the children moved out, the fire department and ambulance personnel replaced them. When I finally returned to the deck to lend assistance, the place was deserted as though nothing had ever happened. The voice of the coach echoed across the room.

"Ruth Anne! Stay with the body and make sure no one else comes in here. Do you understand?"

"Uh, yeah," I remember responding. "Uh, body?"

The coach pointed. There, still lying next to the shallow end of the pool, draped with a white sheet, was the small form of a nine-year-old. The other victim had apparently been revived and rushed off to the hospital. I sat down next to the small boy and we remained alone together in the vacant natatorium for some time.

The sound of a door opening broke the silence. An old woman emerged, walking hesitantly as police officers supported her at each elbow. She resembled a schoolmarm with her spectacles perched atop her nose and white hair arranged neatly in a bun. A cameo topped her white ruffled blouse and a long black skirt tumbled to well below her knees. Square-toed Cuban heels completed the ensemble—classic grandmother without a doubt. The boy's parents were away on business. It was with a firmly clenched jaw that she accepted the responsibility of identification that now fell to her.

There was no conversation, no sound. One officer raised the sheet. The woman's form went limp as she nodded in the affirmative. The sheet was carefully lowered and they left as they had come, slowly and silently.

The wind's force suddenly cut through me as I stood there on the mountain, causing me to shudder uncontrollably. Or, perhaps the shudder was one of cold fear. Death was suddenly a face I was becoming all-too-familiar with. I stayed for a moment longer, gazing at the lifeless form that only hours before had been a living, breathing mountain guide. I squeezed my eyes shut and tried hard to feel Bob's presence. He'd told me he would be sending me warm thoughts while I was on the mountain. If there was ever a time I needed them, it was now.

It occurred to me that here I was, on vacation by choice, but unwittingly off-course and in a battle zone behind enemy lines, caught in the crossfire of a surprise attack. I was beginning to feel as if we were all under siege, clinging to life only because we still managed the strength to keep death at arm's length— but for how much longer?

I headed back to the tent and *The Firm*. Perhaps, in the relative shelter of my sleeping bag I could lose myself in a story of self-conscious yuppies with conflicting ethical issues and country club memberships. If the yuppies couldn't help me, then at least restless sleep should. All I knew was that I needed to be off this mountain for a moment, if only on a fantasy trip.

{7} THE CAPTIVE AUDIENCE

SUNDAY, MAY 17
Day fifteen on the mountain

I t didn't make sense, but I kept dreaming I was speeding along in a car, hitting the brakes hard and catapulting my body forward in a tumbling, accelerating motion. I was aware even of the g forces. Weird! Following one catapult too many, I awoke to the excruciating burn of thawing flesh and smiled. During the night, because I had been careless and rested my feet against the door, they'd frozen again. Craig, ever the gallant one, calmed my immediate panic and wrapped my feet in his parka. Now, though my feet hurt like hell, they were full of feeling, which meant that the flesh was still alive, thank God! I couldn't bear the thought of losing any part of my body, for any reason.

As the pain began chasing the fog from my mind, I became aware of the stale odor of wet down and fleece that hung heavily in the tent. Our once colorful fabric mountain chalet had been reduced to a decaying slum. The only thing missing were hordes of rats and swarms of cockroaches.

"I gotta get out of this scum-suckin' hole of a tent," screamed Craig to no one in particular as he clawed at the tent zipper.

Sticking his head partway out of the door and peering into

the storm, Craig called back to me: "Still blowing. Total white-out. Totally socked in. Completely screwed!"

"Damn. By the feel of it," I said, pounding my fist against the side of the tent, "we're also buried in snow halfway up the tent wall. We gotta dig out."

Craig nodded and, after slipping on his parka, he ducked out of our tent and into the void of swirling white. While Craig worked feverishly outside with the snow shovel, I worked inside scraping all the frost and condensation off the tent's walls with a bowl in an attempt to dry out our musty home. The inside of our tent resembled a freezer badly in need of defrosting. Once all of the walls had been scraped, I scooped up the handfuls of slush that now lay piled up on the floor and tossed them outside. In some places, where the frost had been flaking off without assistance, it had actually managed to form drifts. Directly under our sleeping mats, heated by the warmth of our bodies, the snow and frost had melted, forming puddles, some of them actually quite expansive. Somehow, I had to remove the water since soaked gear is death in this environment. With nothing to really sop or scoop it up, I reached for my knife and installed two workable drains by cutting small slits a few inches long directly under each of our mats. Now our home away from home boasted indoor plumbing. Using my hand as a sort of squeegee, I managed to steer most of the water toward the slits and out of our tent.

Lying there in the tent, gazing up at the dull color of muted light filtering through storm and tent while the fury of the wind beat down on me, I became aware that I was very much balancing on the edge here. The one overwhelming positive to the entire experience thus far was Craig and the fact that he was of a like mind—get up the mountain only if it could be done safely, and get home with our lives and our bodies intact. I couldn't have asked for a better tentmate. Our shared attitude had become one of cautious optimism. We were grateful just to have some food, supplies, a tent, and to be relatively well dug-in. We'd run out of stories to tell, having laughed and cried together for nearly twenty-four hours a day since the storm first hit. In such situations, when two strangers are forced into such an intimate partnership with survival in the balance, you either end up hating each other or being friends for life. So far, we were hanging tough. He had loaned me his bivi sack . . . I was sharing my vitamins with him. Simple gestures, maybe, but up here on the edge of the world, those gestures mean everything. I'd heard of mountaineering couples choosing a Denali adventure as a perfect honeymoon. What a way to wreck a marriage!

"So much for doing carries today," exclaimed Craig as he dove back into the tent accompanied by a torrent of blowing snow. "This is such a joke!"

"Well, I installed plumbing while you were out."

Craig looked at me as if I had finally lost my mind.

"No, really . . . look," as I pointed to the slit under his mat. "I cut one under mine, too. It's the only way to keep the water draining out of here and us relatively dry."

"Wow, a plumber, too? You amaze me."

We both cracked up laughing.

Craig turned, rummaged around in his gear, and emerged clutching the infamous deck of cards.

"Gin, anyone?" Craig inquired while shuffling the well-worn deck.

"Sure, I live to get hammered on by you. . . . Deal them up." We'd already played nearly a bajillion games, but at least it was something to do to take the mind off our claustrophobic and monotonous existence.

In short order, the game was over, yet another mercy killing.

"GIN!" yelled Craig, scattering cards all over the tent. Running his fingers through his hair like a madman, he began to look wildly around the tent.

"Jesus Christ . . . oh man, Ruth Anne, I can't take this. I just *gotta* get outta here."

Leaving me to play 52 Pickup, he bolted outside.

I knew how he felt. I wanted to move around, too, but the pain in my feet and the incredible cold dictated that I remain huddled up under the covers, conserving whatever energy I had for those brief trips to the dining cave or toilet site.

Only about five minutes had passed before Craig hurled himself back inside and practically on top of me. With eyes bugged wide-open he sputtered, "Oh man, if it gets any worse out there, I'm goin' to have to shit right here in a baggie. . . . You okay with that?!"

Far be it for me to come between a man and his personal needs. "Not to worry, Craig. I have no intention of getting in your way."

"While I was out there, I ran into the ranger."

"And?"

"The death toll is officially up to three and a half, no shit."

I propped myself up on my elbow and stared at Craig. "You're joking, right? Three and . . . did you say, one-half?"

"Yep. We've got the guy in the body bag by the med tent, the two Italians—at least, the ranger's still reasonably sure it's the Italians swinging in the wind above camp—and then there's some poor guy who's apparently frozen solid from about mid-thigh on down. . . . Ranger said someone else was going to try to drag him down the mountain on a sled."

"What about the Koreans?" I had been wondering about them ever since we had listened to their cries for help and a helicopter over the radio the last couple of nights. We hadn't heard anything more from them in nearly twenty-four hours. Since the weather hadn't let up, there was no way for a helicopter to make a rescue attempt. For all we knew, they would be adding to the mounting body count before the storm had blown over.

"Didn't hear about them," Craig murmured. "You don't need much of an imagination to guess what is going on up above us, though, poor bastards."

No one had died on Denali the previous year, and now, with the climbing season barely open, we were already up to three fatalities—and probably more.

Wrapped up in the misery of this cold and damp mountain existence, it became commonplace to try to ignore one of mountaineering's most important lessons: Never assume things are so bad that they can't get worse.

"Crevasse! Crevasse!" A screaming voice cut through the storm like a hot blade through butter. My hair even stood on

end. Reality walked up and slapped me hard—things had indeed just gotten worse.

My query about the state of the Korean team was being answered. One of them was staggering back into camp screaming pitifully. His name was Duk Sang Jang, and at his insistence, Ron Johnson, the mountain's rescue ranger, sent four others, including John Roskelley and Jim Wickwire, up the Headwall, in blizzard conditions, to see if anyone was alive.

The tale they told later of what they found when they arrived at the crevasse's lip was chilling—a gaping hole approximately 150 feet long, 50 feet across, and almost 80 feet deep. Hundreds of other climbers had been crossing over this same shelf for the past two weeks, thinking it solid. Even Roskelley admitted, with all his experience, that he, too, thought the shelf was as solid as they come. The Koreans hadn't made a terribly bad decision, just a very unlucky one. In their struggle to return to the relative safety of our camp, they'd stopped on the only flat spot along the trail up to the ridge, and the flat spot had simply caved in. The crevasse itself was filled with a jumbled pile of broken ice blocks and layers of snow, and buried in the middle of it all were two Koreans, one trapped from the waist down, the other, his hand protruding upward.

Roskelley and another rescuer rappelled down and onto what appeared to be the bottom of the crevasse. They could only pray that this layer of ice and snow wouldn't collapse farther into the crevasse with them standing on it. Seong Yu Kang, the Korean buried from the waist down, had attempted to scratch and claw a conical pit around his waist using only a pocket knife, but he was a long way from freeing himself. He'd been trapped now for at least three hours and at an air temperature of minus-15 degrees, was probably freezing to death.

Both Roskelley and the other rescuer dug with a focused energy, intent on getting Kang free while not shaking loose the fragile pile of rubble they were all perched on. Johnson, who had arrived at the scene with a Sked Sled (a heavy, plastic rescue sled), set up a pulley system and helped the team haul up Kang.

While Kang was getting hauled out, Roskelley and the other rescuer turned their attentions to the hand reaching skyward from his arctic tomb. Laboring in an eerie silence punctuated by their heavy breathing, they began cutting ice away from part of the body. It appeared as if the Korean was dead, so they decided to bolt before the entire ice shelf collapsed. It was a difficult decision, but the risk of staying in the crevasse outweighed the benefits in attempting to rescue a dead person. As the rescuer turned to leave, the hand clutched at his ankle. With one grab, the "body" managed to convince its rescuers that their efforts would be worth the trouble.

As they dug, they uncovered Dong Choon Seo's face and he began to scream, horribly. The snow around his head was crimson and blood flowed freely from his mouth. Although Roskelley and the other rescuers didn't know it at the time, blood was flowing because Seo had done the unthinkable. Assuming he was trapped for good in the crevasse and likely to die slowly by freezing, Seo had attempted to chew off his own tongue in an effort to speed up his demise.

After the Sked was lowered again, Roskelley and the other rescuer loaded Seo onto it, wrapping him in a sleeping bag and strapping him in like a trussed package. According to Ranger

Johnson, he used "more duct tape on [him] than I've ever used in my car." With so many injuries, the only items in camp left to make splints of were the trash-can lids—so he used them, too.

They returned to camp later that night. One of the rescuers, eyes vacant and lips pressed into a tight line, referred to the event as "a rescue patrol from hell and the most frightening moun-taineering experience of my life." Even the venerable and un-shakable Roskelley admitted it was the most terrifying thing he'd ever been through. Ranger Johnson, who'd slept only one hour in twenty-four by his own admission, just shook his head, mut-tered something about "having to get the hell off this mountain," and disappeared into his tent. What had happened to the rest of the Korean team was anyone's guess.

While the rescue was going on, things went from bad to worse at camp. Some of the team seemed to be trying to shut out the horror to save what little was left of their sanity. During an afternoon foray outside, I brushed by John just outside our tent. He was staring blankly ahead and shuffling stiffly along, almost as if he were mimicking a robot. There was no acknow-ledgment of my presence or even that John was aware of any-thing at all.

"John?" I called to him.

No answer as he continued to shuffle along, staring vacantly straight ahead.

"*John,* are you okay?" I shouted a little more forcefully.

Still no response.

I got right into his face and screamed at him, "JOHN, ARE YOU OKAY!? ANSWER ME! JOHN!"

He just kept shuffling until he arrived at his tent, ducked, and then disappeared inside. I could only stand there, my mouth agape, and shake my head in wonder. We were all reacting to the stress of the storm's intensity in different ways. Perhaps John had just temporarily shut down for sanity's sake—I hoped.

I retreated again to the relative protective sanctuary of the tent and flopped down, staring first at my watch and then up at the gray light filtering through the rip-stop pattern in the tent fabric. Only two hours until dinner—practically an eternity when wrapped in a cocoon of boredom. Craig was breathing heavily and appeared to have retreated into a world of restful sleep.

Not tired at all, I resigned myself to staring vacantly up into space and letting my mind wander. Soon I was drifting. I found myself lying on the sand on a Maui beach in the shore break with waves of 85-degree water gently lapping over me. Pure bliss. Each time a wave washed over my body, I felt the sand beneath erode away so that, gradually, I became more buoyant and less anchored to the shore. Finally, a wave tugged me with sufficient force to swing my body feetfirst to the right. Only the index finger of my left hand, hooked like a claw into the sand, kept me from drifting out to sea.

"Rak . . . I'm here."

The voice was clear, although even in my subconscious I knew that I couldn't hear anyone that clearly over the raging winds. There was no doubt as to the voice's origin though. It belonged to my best friend, Jan, who had died two months before. Only she had ever called me Rak. So, if she was "here," then where the hell was I?

I shot up, gasping for air with beads of sweat clinging to my face.

Craig, alarmed at my reaction and no longer in lullaby-land, grabbed me forcefully.

"What's wrong!?"

"I must—" I stopped, swallowing hard to slow my gasps. "I must have been having a nightmare. Oh Craig, it really freaked me out."

"Well, that's an understatement. You look as though you've just seen a ghost."

I looked sharply at him. There was no way I could tell him what I'd just experienced. I simply buried the entire event under an avalanche of logic.

"No ghost. My mind's just playing tricks on me—too little sleep, too little food, too much cold, too much of this insanity. I need to get out of this tent. . . . It's dinner anyway. You coming?"

Craig nodded. We never spoke of it again.

As we were crouching down to slide into the dining cave, we heard Franklin screaming.

"Paul, get your ass out here and come to dinner. You have to eat! Don't make me come in there and kick your ass out, goddammit!"

Franklin had become Paul's caretaker. Paul had begun refusing to leave the tent for any reason, refusing to respond to anyone, but Franklin's anger snapped him out of his stupor. He emerged, disheveled and bleary-eyed, and shuffled to dinner.

Team Vern, Jack, and Randy had gone silent and somber, too. Vern had lost his bluster and no longer filled the air with idle chatter and boastings about gear and personal bravado. Randy, ever the quipster, managed only weak attempts at humor and noted this evening that we could take pride in the fact that, with any luck, we might become part of the next Denali park movie, starring as ourselves: starvation victims.

Jack only mumbled about the fact that he had calculated we needed 6,000 calories per day per person if we wanted any chance at the summit and that we didn't stand a chance since we weren't getting anywhere near that amount. We found it strange that he would obsess so much about food and calories, as if that was all that was required to summit a mountain. Of course, Jack had already proven that he would do just about anything for food.

He was often the first in line at meals and usually reluctant to share a tidbit. But Jack wasn't the only one obsessing about food. Early in the climb, we discovered the entire supply of group pilot bread (a thick, hard biscuit) missing. However, when Win confronted the group, everyone denied it and the issue was dropped. As valuable as food was, it wasn't worth eroding the team's dynamics just to ferret out a thief.

After dinner, it became evident that Paul had selected me as his après-dinner conversation companion. He moved over to sit next to me, almost in my lap, and launched into an urgently relayed story. Even though I could feel my feet beginning to freeze again, I sat there, motionless, and listened.

"My mother knows something is wrong . . . she always does. It's uncanny. I think she's psychic. Do you believe in psychics?" Paul's face was inches from mine as he stared into my eyes. He looked a shadow of the triathlete and Iron Man competitor who had begun this climb. His shoulders drooped and he hunched over under the weight of his emotional burden. Gray flecks peppered his thick black beard that did a poor job of hiding the sunken cheeks underneath.

I just nodded and said nothing.

"Well, anyway, I think she is. Hell, she has to be. When I was flying missions in Desert Storm, I had a real close call one day and when I returned to my barracks that night I had a call from my mother. How she figured out where to call me is amazing. She told me that she knew I had been in danger. Said she could feel the fear at the same time I did. Do you think she knows now?"

He was glassy-eyed. Staring into space. I didn't respond—didn't have to. He'd stopped talking to me and was just carrying on a stream-of-consciousness monologue. He kept on rambling, about what I don't recall.

Suddenly he turned and, once again inches from my face, spoke to me.

"Ruth Anne, do you know what my favorite quote is? 'Cherish the present because it will soon be the past, and remember the past because it was once all that was possible.'"

He continued staring at me for a minute, then got up and left without another word. I was left sitting alone, in a darkened cave, dreading the return to my tent. This present wasn't one to be cherished at all.

MONDAY, MAY 18
Day sixteen on the mountain

It was three A.M. and nature was calling, loudly. I groaned, got dressed, and crawled outside to do my morning squat. As I crouched just a few feet away from the tent with my backside bare to the stinging onslaught of wind, I became acutely aware that, directly overhead, the sky was clear. Not a cloud. Strange to see blue sky above but be able to see nothing to either side. The ground blizzards were still going ballistic. I had to brace myself on the ground to keep from being blown over and rolled away. Mountaineering wouldn't be half as bad if it weren't for having to drop trou and go to the bathroom in any conditions.

After battening down my personal hatches, I began to crawl back to the tent. I could feel the intensity of the wind pick up and then my body sliding backward over the snow. I clung to the mountain with my fingers and toes for all I was worth, pressed my body as low as possible and began to work my way inch by inch toward the tent door. I genuinely believe that if I had raised myself up to a standing position, I would have become airborne.

As I slipped back inside, I realized that, because of the racket from the wind, Craig had slept through and never heard me leave. Not a comforting thought imagining that, like a tiny dust speck, I could have been blown from the mountain without anyone knowing. I retreated from the onslaught by curling up into a ball inside my sleeping bag.

The next thing I knew, Craig was up on one elbow and bent over my face.

"Do ya hear that?"

"Hear what! All I hear is the goddamn wind, Craig. . . . Go back to sleep."

"No, listen! It's an airplane."

"You're dreaming. There is no way you could hear anything over this racket."

"No . . . no, I hear it. It's a plane, I know it. I've got to get out there and wave so that they know we're alive." He was wild-eyed and dressed only in long underwear as he lunged for the door.

I threw myself in front of him, blocking his escape. "Craig! Where on earth do you think you're going? Get a grip, man! You can't go out there. If a plane is flying overhead, it'll never see you. I was out there earlier . . . it was horrible, terrifying. Besides, you're not even dressed."

"Get out of my way. I'm not going to die for this damn mountain." Craig had worked himself into full panic mode, a wild man high on adrenaline and fear, trying to move me out of his way.

"If you go out there right now, you *will* DIE," I screamed into his face.

He rocked back onto his haunches and buried his head into his clenched fists. "I just can't take any more of this. I've got to get out of the tent."

"Look, I hear the engine, too, which means things must be improving and they know we're alive. We have to be patient."

Just then, the engine trailed off. We waited, breathless, but it never came back. Feeling like lost souls, Craig and I stared at each other in silence.

By mid-afternoon the weather had broken. Brilliant sunlight cast a glow of warmth, however superficial, over the entire camp. While there were still high winds above us and gusting winds around us at camp, it was tolerable enough to remain outside, and go outside we did. Everyplace I looked, heads were popping out of tent flaps, bearing ear-to-ear grins.

This was the first time I'd actually seen our surroundings since the storm descended on us, and what I saw was spectacular. Clouds hung below us, like a fluffy sea of gray and white stretching away from camp. Other clouds cascaded in wispy streams over the ridges of Mount Foraker. Above us, clouds and snow swirled around the upper flanks of Denali, demonstrating that, while it might be sunny where we were, up above the weather was anything but pleasant. Several search planes circled high above, tiny silver dots against a backdrop of deep blue. Although three of the Koreans had been rescued, there was no word regarding the fate of the other six, still trapped on the mountain above. Some were still alive, that we knew. Each night, listening to the radio, we could hear their plaintive cries for help. If they were dying, it was slowly.

I ran into Robert during my first unsteady lap around camp. He confirmed something strange certainly was going on above us because of the airplane circling camp earlier. What exactly was up, he didn't know. He hadn't been told nor did he expect to be told.

"Do you think they're trying to find the Koreans?"

"I would imagine that is certainly one of their goals," said Robert in a matter-of-fact tone.

I nodded and wondered aloud why it seemed that Asians were the ones to suffer most on many of the world's mountains.

Robert shrugged. "I think it's because they always appear to be in a hurry. They almost seem to have a suicidal approach which appears to be borne out by the very high record of casualties on their climbs."

I continued walking laps around camp, trying to regain my strength and help my feet. I felt like a high-altitude Walter Cronkite, pacing in circles, talking into my microcassette. My cassette, which had been with me on every mountain and knew my every thought and fear, had become my surrogate confessor.

I could tell it anything and whisper the unspeakable, not to mention the unthinkable.

As I walked, I noticed that the advanced basecamp was thinning out quickly. Several teams were packing up and leaving for lack of food. Others were simply running because they were demoralized. Those that remained were, like us, wandering about, trying to recover their senses after the storm's onslaught and waiting to see if things stabilized. There was one constant through the varying emotions, however—no one dared hazard an attempt to climb higher on the mountain just yet.

Suddenly, like a scene from a B-grade war movie, a helicopter roared up and over the ice shelf, materializing almost from thin air. It skimmed over the tents and landed next to the medical tent where it picked up its cargo—one of the Koreans injured in the mouth of Jaws the day before. Then, just as quickly as it appeared, the helicopter lifted off, levitated sideways over the glacier, and dropped out of sight.

"Ruth Anne!"

Even with my parka hood acting as a blinder, I'd recognize that voice anywhere.

"Ruth Anne," the voice gasped breathlessly next to me.

"Yes, Paul?"

"Did you see that?! Wow!"

Something told me I was in for an impromptu tutorial on helicopters.

"That, Ruth Anne, was a Llama helicopter. There are only three in the world. I can't believe I just saw one." Paul was so excited he was practically jumping up and down.

Gesturing toward the place where the helicopter had first

appeared, Paul gushed on. "They can fly to over twenty thousand feet, the only helicopter that can do that. They're French, you know. Did you see how stripped down it was, so he could get high like this? That was incredible!"

Very little time passed before the sky jockey returned, now fighting the surging, swirling winds above us in an attempt to land on a narrow rock outcropping. The entire camp held its collective breath as the tiny helicopter was bounced and tossed all over the sky, rather like a hanging Christmas ornament being batted around by a playful kitten. One minute we'd see the tiny craft, the next it would disappear in the churning clouds. One moment the pilot appeared to be attempting a landing, the next a wild retreat. Each time, the helicopter would bank toward the rocks, then pull sharply away—in and out, up and down. It was impossible for those of us on the ground to predict which direction the pilot would come from or go to next as the winds tossed the helicopter about. I began to get the horrible feeling that I was about to witness something I really didn't want to see.

Finally, in one aggressively amazing move, the pilot wrestled his steed into the wind and held it as steadily as he could just above the rocks. With all the snow churned up by the rotary blades, it was hard to tell if he was on the ground or just hovering. We watched as a figure was loaded quickly into the copter. One of the other figures tried to hang what looked to be a pack on the helicopter's runners, but the pilot kicked it off. Then the helicopter surged upward, banked, swooped down, and landed at the medical tent.

Like witnesses to a particularly gory highway accident, members of our camp gathered as near as we dared and watched the ranger and another person run out of the medical tent to greet the helicopter. It took both of them to carry the single passenger inside. From my vantage point near the tent door, I could see that it was one of the Koreans. His bare hands and face were completely black from frostbite. His eyes, bright white against an inky black skin, were vacant and hollow. He was alive, but his mind had checked out. I shuddered.

I was so engrossed in staring at this apparition that I failed to notice the pilot had come and gone and was returning again, with yet another victim. Like the first, two people were required to carry him into the tent. Also like the first, his goggles and sunglasses were long gone but unlike the other, his eyes, white against the darkness of frozen and dying skin, rolled this way and that, as if searching for a reason to explain this current state of affairs.

Once more, flying into the teeth of the wind, the pilot took off, plucking a third Korean out of the mountain's icy grip. Like the other two, he was a nightmarish apparition—white eyes, black skin, confused state of mind.

Just as quickly as he had arrived, and carrying another of the injured Koreans rescued the day before, the quiet hero piloted his craft toward the edge of the ice shelf and then dove downward, clawing for solid ground with soft green grass and more stable air.

With three Koreans rescued yesterday and three plucked from death's embrace today, only three more remained unaccounted for. Where were they? My eyes searched the ridges above camp, for what, I didn't know. If the Koreans were still alive and still above us, they'd be invisible to me—too much swirling snow and clouds.

"Ruth Anne! Look."

It was Paul again, calling excitedly my way and pointing in the direction of Talkeetna.

My eyes scanned the horizon in the direction he was pointing and soon I picked out another helicopter heading our way, this one much larger than the first. After days of being unable to see a thing, we had front-row seats to an air show.

"It's a Pavehawk. The Air National Guard flies them."

Why Paul had to tell me this, I have no idea. All I cared was that it was a really, really big helicopter. The name meant nothing.

As it got closer, it seemed to be doing more lumbering than flying. The thing was a dinosaur. We scattered as it hovered next to the medical tent, kicking up a miniature snow storm. The helicopter dwarfed the medical tent and everything in camp around it—rather like having a large house land.

The ranger ushered the first of the Koreans out of the medical tent and toward the helicopter. Without warning, the Korean turned and began to punch the ranger, screaming and yelling at him. The same burly fellow who had helped the ranger carry the Koreans from the first helicopter into the medical tent jumped into the fray and slapped the Korean in a headlock, dragging him toward the Pavehawk. Just as soon as they unceremoniously dumped the kicking and screaming Korean into the helicopter, he attempted to jump back out. Fortunately, for the Korean, someone inside the helicopter stopped him. I say fortunately, because if he had jumped out, there was a gathering crowd of mountaineers who would have been all too glad to kick his butt on principle alone.

We watched as the scene repeated itself with each of the remaining Koreans. This was certainly an original way to show appreciation. Had the Llama pilot not risked his life to save these three who had been trapped on Cassin Ridge, they would have surely died. They'd been without food and water for nearly a week. Worse, the storm had blown away their tent, their clothes, and extra gear.

"Why'd they kick up such a fuss?" I asked the wearied and bruised ranger standing next to the medical tent.

"Those sons of bitches! When that pilot pulled each one of them off the ridge, the conditions were too wild for him to fully touch down and his loads had to be kept to an absolute minimum or he'd have never made it. That meant he had to rescue each climber individually and he didn't have the extra cushion to add the weight of their packs to the load."

"You mean they were throwing a tantrum just because they had left their packs behind?" I was incredulous as I thought back to when I saw the pilot kick that object off his helicopter's runners.

"You got it. Those bastards were insisting that the pilot be made to fly back up there to pick up their gear before they'd board the Pavehawk. Go figure. I don't think they ever did say thanks to anyone, either." With that, the ranger wearily ducked inside the medical tent and disappeared.

I stood there, stunned into silence. I couldn't be sure under what mountaineers' code the Koreans operated, but I knew for certain that if it came down to a choice between me and my gear, I'd leave my gear without hesitation. I also knew that I'd be undyingly grateful for anyone who had risked their life to save mine.

My eyes rested on the Swiss guide's body bag, still lying unattended, next to the tent. There would be no rescue for him, although I had no doubt that he would have happily traded his gear for a few more years on this earth. The mountain had taken his life, yet had spared the lives of the Koreans. Somehow, it didn't seem fair.

With conditions improving and the coming and going of helicopters, a polarity began to develop within our little group. As we sat around that evening drinking hot cocoa, John, Vern, and Jack spoke more earnestly than they had several days ago of wanting to use this opportunity to flee the mountain. Franklin, Craig, Randy, and I remained committed to the climb. Paul remained silent on the issue. Robert and Win listened, then Robert spoke.

"We've been down this road before, gang. I remind all of you that we're safe and we've got sufficient provisions to either continue on to the summit or retreat. We will not, I repeat, will not take any unnecessary risks." Robert's voice was level and firm, his eyes searching out the eyes of each member of the group as he spoke. "However, we cannot afford to weaken the team by having just a few go down the mountain. Whatever we do, we do as a team."

"Now, I know Franklin, Craig, Randy, and Ruth Anne have already stated that they want to go up, not down, is that right?" We all nodded in agreement.

"Okay, what about you Paul?"

I stared at Paul intently. He knew how I felt, how Craig felt, because I'd told him. There is no mountain in this world worth dying for, if you look at it framed in an overly simplistic

black-and-white picture. No one goes to a mountain to die—
that's stupid. Yes, climbing and mountaineering are dangerous
and every task, every step, is a calculated risk. So is getting in a
car and driving to work. You weigh your skills and assets against
the challenges and if the stack comes up weighted on the skills-
and-assets side, you forge ahead. If not, you leave. In this case,
going down was just as hazardous as going up, and we were in
no immediate danger as I saw it. True, my priorities had swayed
from simply getting to the top no matter what, to one of getting
off the mountain safely. But if we could summit and get off the
mountain safely, then why not at least try for the summit? It
seemed ridiculous to me to retreat out of blind fear. We were
fine right here and still had a shot and I knew in my heart that
if we didn't at least try, we would all live to regret that call. To
me, the decision to stay or retreat was a nondecision—we should
stay—but it was not my call to make alone. I sat on the edge
of the ice bench and awaited their answers.

Paul blinked and looked around the cave before replying:
"I'm happy with whatever the group decides. I figure we've
come this far, we might as well press on."

"Good. John?"

John looked right at me, as if probing the inner shadows of
my mind before answering with a deep breath: "I'll be honest,
I expected this climb to last seventeen days at most, and I'd go
down today given the chance, but if the group wants to go up,
then I'll go up."

"Good enough. Vern?"

"As I've told you all before, I *am* expected back at work on
Tuesday."

"You're not going to be back on Tuesday, Vern. Now, how do you feel about going on?"

Vern looked around the room, seeking an ally who would encourage his need to escape. He found none. Shoulders slumping, he replied, "I guess they can get along without me."

"Fine. Jack?"

"Like Vern, I was supposed to be back at work, too, but I'll stay."

"Outstanding. So let's focus on getting up this mountain and stop all the mumbling about wanting to get off, Okay? Okay! Let's whip up some dinner. You'll need the fuel for tomorrow's carry to 16,500 feet."

If all went well, we would summit in three days, making us one of the first expeditions to reach the top after the recent tragedies. Assuming no weather challenges, that meant we could expect to be winging our way home in less than a week.

Win and Robert moved the cookstoves outside.

"No sense in eating indoors when we can dine with a view," quipped Win.

Like refugees, we milled around the stoves while Win spooned the evening slop into our bowls. I watched Jack, who had been first in line as always, wolf his ration down and then slink back to the stoves and hold his bowl out for more.

Craig nudged me. "Can you believe him?"

I just stared.

Win was just about to ladle another load into Jack's bowl when he looked up.

"You've already had yours, haven't you?" His tone was firm, more of an accusation than a question.

Jack nodded.

"Well then, you've had all you're getting. This food has gotta go to someone who hasn't eaten yet."

Jack just shrugged and plopped down in the snow next to Vern, who was still sampling his fare.

I looked away to hide my growing rage from Craig and anyone else who might be looking my way. I worked to focus on the beauty that surrounded me instead of Jack's selfishness.

All around, hues of pink washed the sky and melded into the soft blue shadow of the earth cast against the atmosphere. Pink and purple clouds, reflecting the light from the sky, poured off Foraker's shoulders like an elegant velvet cape. Its summit wore a hat of lenticulars, stacked five deep.

The ranger stopped by, having grabbed just a few hours of rest. Apparently, one of the other teams had spotted a trail of debris down a chute ominously named the Orient Express. Since no one had been able to investigate yet, the ranger wanted to be sure everyone in camp was accounted for.

"Perhaps we now know what has happened to the other three Koreans," said Craig quietly.

"I suspect you're right, there," replied the ranger solemnly.

We ate the rest of our meal in silence. It seemed strange to be eating outdoors without the thunderous backdrop of wind. After so many days of tumult, the quiet seemed almost unsettling. I began to wonder what the mountain had in store for us next.

{8} BREAKING THROUGH TO THE OTHER SIDE

—◆—

Day seventeen on the mountain

There was no way I could tolerate another night like the last one. My feet were in excruciating pain. My toes felt as if they were going to burn off my feet and my soles felt as if someone were pressing a hot branding iron against my flesh. They hurt continually now, which was fine during the day when I had enough to distract me, but at night, when sleep was all there was, the pain became unbearable. Motrin had become my best friend, and, at times, I felt as though I were popping the tiny little pills like breath mints—anything to make the burning go away.

Against my better judgment, I fumbled through my gear and found my mirror. I didn't recognize the person looking back at me. There was no cheerful glint, only a deeply furrowed forehead and sunken eyes framed by black circles. Smooth skin had been replaced by raw flesh, the result of perpetual sandblasting by wind-driven ice particles. The soft, warm lips, the kind my husband used to love kissing, were gone, too. Instead, strips of cracked and bleeding meat with bits of skin dangling loosely here and there had taken their place.

"Lookin' good, Ruth Anne." Craig, whose face looked as weather-beaten as mine, was smiling broadly.

I managed a grin back, although I felt my lips cracking with the effort.

"So, Mr. *GQ*, who does your hair?" His hat had come off during the morning wrestle to get dressed, revealing the same Medusa locks we all sported. Since we hadn't seen a bar of soap or a drop of bathing water in weeks, we were very glad our significant others were unable to witness our physical deterioration.

"Man, I need a vacation from my vacation," said Craig, while fingering his battered face. "I think I've aged twenty years in just two weeks."

I nodded. The thought hadn't escaped me that this punishing coexistence could be taking years off our lives. At a minimum, we were certainly losing our minds.

"It would be nice to be warm and pampered right now, wouldn't it?" My thoughts drifted to Bob and his belief that the only good climb is one that ends in a hot tub. What I wouldn't give to be soaking in a hot tub with him now.

"I should be at home in Minnesota sitting on the pier drinking mai-tais. By the time we get out of here, I'll barely have enough strength left to lift an empty glass," Craig moaned.

He was right. Altitude and cold were eating us alive. We were wasting away. I couldn't help but imagine that our next steps up the mountain would be like beginning a difficult climb after an extensive stay in the hospital with no chance for rehab.

Craig and I sat quietly staring at each other, without really looking at each other. Our brief hiatus of the day before had proved to be an illusory calm. The all-too-familiar roar of the wind had returned, eclipsing the sliver of peace I had begun to grasp for, and replacing it with foreboding.

"The wind . . . it's back with a vengeance," Craig said quietly, turning his gaze from mine and moving toward the door.

"Maybe it's just a result of residual instability and it'll blow over soon."

"Do you really believe that?"

"No, but without some hope, there's really no reason to continue, is there?"

Craig nodded and ducked out the door to begin packing for the climb.

Wind or no wind, we were preparing to carry our loads up to 16,500 feet. First we had to locate all the necessary gear that had been left frozen and dormant for the past eight days. All our packs, harnesses, and ropes were buried, frozen stiff, and had to be broken loose from the mountain's grasp. We checked ascenders, crampons, and ice axes to be sure they worked after being entombed in layers of snow and ice. We laid out loads and divided them equally. Finally, we took steps to secure our camp to ensure that it would be here when we returned. That meant repairing ice-block walls, stowing gear and sleds, and securing tents. Although we'd be gone only twelve hours or so, that would be more than enough time for the weather to change twelve times and blast apart our tenuous hold on the mountain.

Finally we each clipped into the knots tied at 25-foot intervals on one of the two ropes that Robert and Win had laid out, and began to climb. Thankfully, the first five hundred feet of climbing was gradual, following a sweeping traverse up toward the fixed lines (ropes secured semipermanently into the ice that act rather like handrails or safety lines on steep terrain). I had just enough time to convince my screaming muscles that there was no cause for alarm and that they had better start working together because, dammit, this was not a democracy and they didn't get a vote—I was going up whether they protested or not. Just as the first fixed line snuck up on us, I found my rhythm, although not my strength.

There was no turning back. Two thousand feet of vertical ice and snow loomed above with fixed lines stretching up as far as the eye could see. The beauty of being on a rope is that once you are tied into it, everything becomes a collective decision. The rope takes on a life of its own—it stops, you stop; it moves, you move. One by one we each reached the fixed line and clipped our ascenders into it, calling out, "Anchor!" to alert the others on the rope to hold up. Then we'd call, "Anchor on!" as soon as we were secured and ready to move up. Since each fixed line was approximately 100 feet in length, we'd have to unclip, calling, "Anchor off!" and then repeat the process all over again.

This grueling, exhausting, and frustrating stop-start procession continued all day long. I could never find a climbing rhythm and the weight of my pack just ground into my shoulders and hips. The route was so steep that I could look up and see the bottom of Robert's crampons ahead of me. If I stood up too straight, I risked tumbling backward, pulled that way by the load in my pack. I stayed on the front points of my crampons and balanced on the toes of my feet most of the day, relying on my ice ax to anchor me every time we stopped.

While the sun felt good on my back, the headwall reflected

its intensity like a mirror right back into my face. I could feel my skin cooking even under layers of zinc and a face shield. Occasionally I'd sneak a glance back down the wall to the ice shelf and our home-away-from-home. There I could pick out the bright red dot of the medical tent and the four orange dots that comprised our camp. Sheltered from the force of the wind, there was little noise to accompany us other than the crunch of snow, the clinking of hardware, and the buzz of search planes circling overhead like vultures, looking for dead or dying climbers.

After hours of climbing we reached our cache site and were immediately blasted by the raw wind tearing across the ridge. Instantly, and as a unit, we dropped to the ice, sank our axes as deeply as we could, and hung on for dear life. The wind plucked and pulled at us, buffeting our team like tiny bits of sand clinging to the beach in the face of an offshore storm. Paul, who had been lifted momentarily into the air, was obviously shaken, and kept screaming, "Oh God, Oh God," over and over until his fear passed and shock took over.

Win and Robert worked swiftly in the face of the wind, digging a pit to bury our supplies. It didn't take long for each of us to offload what we had carried and for Robert to cover it and mark the area with a wand. Speed was of the essence. None of us wanted to spend any longer up here than we had to.

"We won't be climbing tomorrow unless these winds subside some," screamed Robert to me over the wind.

I nodded. Although I felt a tinge of disappointment at again having to delay the summit attempt, climbing in this wind would be suicidal. We had withstood enough punishment already.

Our retreat to camp took us back the way we had come, descending the steep vertical wall while again secured to the fixed line. As I worked my way carefully downward, I looked up from my crampons and feet long enough to spot a stream of other climbers working their way up the same headwall. Our move had triggered a copycat reaction, which didn't really surprise me. Robert's decision-making skills on mountains around the world were highly respected and if other leaders saw Robert and his team going somewhere, they might take that to mean they should be going, too. The trouble with that reaction, however, is that they were working with only partial information. Yes, Robert had decided to go up, but only to cache food and gear. By the looks of the loads these other climbers were schlepping, it appeared as if they had every intention of going up to stay.

I could see Robert staring at them, too, and shaking his head. "Bad move?" I yelled down to him.

He looked back up over his shoulder at me and yelled, "Stupid move! The storm's not done with us yet."

Back at 14,000 feet, camp had virtually emptied out. Some, as we had seen, had elected to go up. Others had joined the exodus from camp begun the day before. The highly publicized team of international climbers, featured on CNN the night before I departed for this climb, had bailed. I felt a sense of smug satisfaction that we had outlasted them.

I felt more sympathy for another group who started out of camp shortly after we had returned. They'd simply run out of food. Giving up their goal of reaching the summit was especially painful to each member of the team since they had been climbing to draw attention to a rare condition called Batton's disease. Their leader told me two of his three children had the disease and wouldn't live past the age of ten. They'd received limited funding and had hoped to place a list of all the children in the world who have the deadly condition on the summit, establishing Denali as a monument to the disease and its need for recognition.

I promised to carry the list to the summit and install it there for them. It seemed to be a small consolation. The leader handed me the list, encased in a green plastic capsule hung on a string. I placed it around my neck and, as I pressed my hand warmly into his, I swore to the leader that Craig and I would photograph it on top and send them the picture, so they'd know that the Batton Kid's climb didn't fail after all. He smiled, choked back his tears, nodded, turned, and headed down the mountain without saying a word. He didn't have to. One of the others in the group thanked me before heading down himself and handed me an extra roll of toilet paper they'd been hoarding—a rare commodity since our climb had extended itself. Greater appreciation they couldn't have shown. I had the feeling that I might be able to sell it one square at a time if we ended up being stuck here much longer.

As I walked back to the tent, Craig caught up with me.

"You know, Ruth Anne, it's moments such as this that I really—no, let me emphasize—really, really, appreciate being your tentmate." Craig was laughing as I clutched the roll of paper.

Glancing over my shoulder at him, I quipped, "I'd hate to think that you are just using me for my toilet paper."

Back at the tent, I fumbled with and then cursed at the tent zipper. Craig just burst out laughing.

"Okay, slick, you try it," I fired back through clenched teeth.

While the temperature had warmed to a blistering zero degrees, producing a mild heat wave, the change brought a new set of problems to contend with. Frozen pellets now shot through the air, glazing everything with a thick crusting of ice and making zippered tent doors virtually impossible to open.

Craig grunted and cursed as he struggled with the zipper. It was my turn to laugh. "Fun, isn't it?"

"Very funny. . . . Either hand me a blowtorch or get me a knife."

"Patience, Craig, patience."

It took about five minutes, but we eventually gained access to our tent without having to burn or cut our way inside.

Retorts highlighted the evening menu once again. We believed we could stretch our food for six more days, but if that meant eating retorts six more times, I really didn't care. The only way to stomach these vile creations was to think of them more as fuel than as food. I'd suck them quickly past my taste buds, let them fall heavily into my stomach, go to bed, and then spend the night trying to forget I ever ate them.

While we were eating and listening to the evening's disaster program, we heard of Mugs Stump's death. Though it was clear he didn't want to show it, Robert had a hard time fighting back tears. Mugs was one of his closest friends and rated as one of the most experienced and accomplished mountaineers in America. The details were sketchy, but from what we heard, it appeared that Mugs had fallen into a crevasse while retreating off the other side of the mountain with his clients. A snow bridge had collapsed, sending him down into blackness and almost taking his team with him. His clients tried in vain to locate him under tons of debris.

Win flicked the radio off and placed a hand on Robert's shoulder. No one said anything more during dinner. As I thought of Mugs and listened to the muffled wind howling outside our snow cave, I wondered how the climbers now struggling to stay alive at 16,500 feet, the ones who had followed us up today, were feeling. The teams above us were clearly in harm's way. Beginning their ascent late in the day would make retreat difficult. The technical route was steep, windswept, and exposed. Happy for the security of our camp here at 14,000 feet, I winced at the possibility that many more might die before this storm subsided—needless deaths, all.

WEDNESDAY, MAY 20
Day eighteen on the mountain

Last night a woman came to visit me in my dreams. She stood just out of my reach holding warm blankets and beckoning to me. I have no doubt in my mind that I was looking at death—in this case a seductress, teasing, enticing. It's difficult to deny the alluring quality of the situation. I wondered if the Swiss guide had seen the same woman and decided to accept her offer of warmth. I am beginning to believe that existence on earth isn't limited to a solid state. There's a transitional place, a real place— a gray area, if you will—where life and death are closer than I'd previously imagined. Here, on this mountain, I felt as if I were constantly straddling the line between the two. Maybe too much has been made of the distinction between life and death. Maybe it's only a subtle transition. Maybe there's nothing really to fear . . . maybe.

We awakened to another storm, or maybe it was the same one—not that defining which storm we were embroiled in really mattered. The bottom line was we were doomed to spend yet another day banished to the confines of our fabric prison.

Craig needed fewer fingers to calculate our dwindling supplies. As of tomorrow, we'd have to make the decision either to go up or down because we would have stretched our food stores to the absolute breaking point. If we went up, it would be with the intention of summiting. Otherwise, we'd position ourselves for a run to basecamp and the flight out. Either way, we'd have to climb back up to 16,500 feet to retrieve our food cache.

Weather forecasts had become a bad joke, so even the rumor circulating around camp that an Army report stated Friday would be clearing was treated as pure conjecture. Of course, if the report was true, we would need to be positioned higher up the mountain by then to have a realistic shot at the summit. Since arriving on Denali, there had been exactly three periods of visibility amounting to half a day each. By now I had adopted the Doors tune "Break On Through to the Other Side" as the group's theme song. I think Craig was getting sick of hearing me muddle through the verses time and again.

Both Craig and I had made a clear distinction between wet and dry camping. We had decided that, as long as it was warm damp, it was okay. If it was frozen damp, it wasn't okay. It was always damp—first frozen damp and then melting damp. At least now we could get our water bottles to partially thaw by carrying them around in the inside pocket of our parkas. For the past few days, even sleeping with the bottles hadn't kept them thawed. And my husband complains about my cold feet. "Try sleeping with a block of ice," I wanted to tell him now.

Meals had ceased to be joyous occasions, especially today. With our supplies cached above, dinner was prepared from the last food available in camp, other than a few candy bars and a few stray packages of Cream of Wheat. The entrance to our dining cave was now so drifted with snow that I had to lie flat on my back to slide in, banking off the walls like a luger making an Olympic run. We all sat quietly, crammed into the dark recess like sardines. Icicles, the remains of this morning's beverage, lined my mug. Win heated the meal, instant mashed potatoes, while we held our empty bowls with outstretched arms. Like Oliver and his orphaned chums in Charles Dickens's classic tale, we gratefully accepted the sloppy white mush he plopped unceremoniously into our bowls. As I finished wolfing down the tasteless slop, I had to fight the temptation to hold out my bowl again and ask, "Please, sir, may I have some more?"

"What do you think Roskelley and Wickwire are up to now?" asked John through mouthfuls of food, shattering the silence that hung heavily in the cave.

We'd seen them climbing up to 16,500 feet the day before and Robert knew that they were planning to bivouac—sleep without tents in waterproof bivi sacks pulled over sleeping bags, sometimes in snow caves.

"Don't really know," mused Robert. "They're experienced enough to pull it off, but without tents and in this weather . . . if they try to summit today, I'll bet they live to regret it."

"Heard anything about the other teams who went up last night?" chimed in Craig.

"Mmm, yeah." Robert wiped a smear of potato from his beard. "The Dutch team came straggling in from above early this morning, very grateful to be alive. Their camp had been ripped apart by the force of the storm—ice walls collapsed on them, tents shredded by the wind, gear swept away into the night. They're on their way down the mountain now, hoping to get flown off from basecamp without delay."

"Sweet Jesus," muttered Paul.

Without warning, chunks of our roof started falling on us. Were we now being subjected to an earthquake, too? Sitting nearest the door, I bolted out with Craig on my heels and came face-to-face with two newcomers digging in the roof of our cave.

"What in the hell are you thinking!?" I screamed at them.

The one mumbled something about getting clean snow to melt for water.

"Don't you see the wands marking the cave, or the chimney right in front of your face?"

I was livid.

"Oh, yeah, we saw the wands, but it didn't occur to us that it meant anything," said the other.

I wanted to slug him.

"Look, man, we're sorry. You know we're only here for a short bit and needed water quickly. We're heading up the Messner Route first thing tomorrow morning."

I looked at both of these idiots and wanted to say something, but just couldn't find the words. First off, the Messner Route is the most difficult one up the mountain and doable only in perfect conditions. Second, even world-renowned mountaineers like Roskelley and Wickwire were sticking to the safer main route. Losers like this doing the Messner Route? *No way!*

Craig, picking up on my amazement fired back sarcastically, "Yeah, right. Why don't you just beat it while we still have a cave left and you can still walk."

"Fucking morons," Craig mumbled as they sauntered off.

THURSDAY, MAY 21
Day nineteen on the mountain

Something cold and wet hit my face, waking me with a start. I wiped slush from my face then glanced upward to discover the source. Giant frost feathers, two to three inches long clung to the ceiling like so many fuzzy stalactites. The inside of our tent was beginning to take on the appearance of a Jules Verne setting. One of the flakes must have fallen on me, shaken loose by the flapping tent, shaking and shuddering under the bludgeoning of a relentless wind.

I elbowed Craig. "What do you think, isn't mountaineering fun?"

He rolled over, glared at me, and then spat, "Shitty tent, shitty weather, shitty trip . . . I hate this. I feel as though I'm on an endless journey to nowhere."

Craig was becoming testy, a justifiable malevolence in caged animals submitted to mental torture. As a diversion, we took to measuring heart rates. Mine clocked at 49, his a few beats higher. We'd spent ample time acclimatizing, although this had to be the first time anyone had spent so long acclimatizing for a descent.

Listening to the wind howling outside, I felt as though the final nail had been driven into the coffin sealing our fate. I couldn't see how we were ever going to get a shot at the summit now. We sat up in the tent and listened in silence. There was no need to rush to get up. We wouldn't be going anyplace soon. Our time was running out. An oppressive sense of powerlessness gripped us. The vertical arena has a habit of reminding climbers that they are not really in control of their world, but here, on the ice shelf, the lesson was a difficult one to swallow.

I shuffled over to the medical tent after performing the compulsory tent excavation, after the night's snow buildup, and ice-wall repair. I'd thought to take a peek at the library the tent was rumored to have inside, but balked at having to walk past a stack of empty body bags and then over the orange bag containing the Swiss guide, so outside I stayed. The ranger was standing next to the entrance with Win, who greeted me with surprising enthusiasm.

"Morning, Ruth Anne. And how are we today?"

I smiled. "Just fine, Win. A little claustrophobic, but basically just fine."

"That's what I like about you, you're always smiling."

I thought to myself, You bet I'm smiling . . . I'm still alive. But I didn't say that to Win. "Well, I'm still here with a shot at the summit and that's reason enough to smile. What have you heard?"

"Well, there's not much of a weather window, if that's what you mean. Still, we've got to go up tomorrow to retrieve our cache, so keep your fingers crossed."

"Oh, they're crossed all right. Heard anything of the other Koreans or anyone else stuck above us?"

The ranger nodded. "Most everyone else is pinned down above. No one is moving. We have spotted the Koreans, though, at the bottom of the Orient Express. That debris trail was from them for certain. Weird, though, that their teammates, the ones still alive, will return to Korea to face charges for the loss of these three. Each of them will have to make an official explanation to their government and to the families of the victims. Sometimes I just don't understand other cultures."

"Me neither," I offered. It was ironic that they had died falling down the chute dubbed the Orient Express. Perhaps it was because they just climbed too recklessly or perhaps it was because they underestimated the mountain. Of course, the reasons really didn't matter. All that mattered was that they were now dead.

I glanced over at the body bags stacked next to the tent. Before long, the Swiss guide wouldn't be alone. He'd have three companions for his final helicopter ride off the mountain.

As I wandered back to our tiny compound I ran into Paul and recounted what I'd heard about the weather and the Koreans.

He just shook his head. "You know, here we are, dug in on a natural battlefield surrounded by carnage. I've been in combat and I can tell you that this is the closest thing going to paying for the privilege of being at war."

Truer words had never been spoken. Our expectations had been denied, our dreams crushed, and our best efforts thrown back at us like worthless fluff. We were, for all practical purposes, on a holiday in hell. Our time on the mountain could not really be described as a brush with death, but rather a close examination of it. We were under siege, on death row . . . waiting.

By mid-afternoon the clouds lifted, creating kaleidoscopic patterns on the mountainside. More people had begun to arrive in camp from other camps below, each hopeful of a successful summit bid. We were quite certain, though, that none of them had suffered as we had and none of them deserved the summit more than we.

Just as the clearing weather allowed us to dream of the summit, evening winds returned to dash our hopes against the rocks of denial. The mountain was playing cruel tricks on us, teasing us with possibility before yanking it away as yet another evil deception. Our future seemed nonexistent, our past a blur of fading memory. We remained mired in the endless moment, searching for a little slice of light to lead us out of the dark tunnel.

At dinner, we consumed the last of what were termed "the stretchables"—heavily watered-down Cream of Wheat, crumbled bits of crackers, broken pieces of candy bars, and a few odd hard candies.

The last few nights, we had listened to the radio and heard reports about us being carried on all the major news networks around the country and the world. All eyes were on the mountain—wondering, speculating on those who had died and those who hadn't. And here we sat, helpless, part of the news, yet unable to do anything about it.

Knowing that our families would be at home worrying and wondering if any of us were among the victims, especially since we were now overdue, Robert called the radio operator in basecamp and requested that they forward a message to each of our families via the park service. While I was grateful that the park service would be contacting families to let them know we were fine, I suspected that those picking up the phone on the other end and hearing, "Hello, this is the Denali National Park Service," might find themselves less relieved and more in need of cardiopulmonary resuscitation. A call from the park service was probably the last phone call anyone wanted to receive right now.

There was no doubt left in my mind: Hell had frozen over.

{9} STAIRWAY TO HEAVEN

FRIDAY, MAY 22
Day twenty on the mountain

S hit . . . I can't believe this!"
  Craig's frustration cut through the early-morning fog in my mind, shaking me out of a shadowy state inspired by the almost hypnotic roaring of the wind and the hiss of blowing snow.

"I know. I've been lying here for hours just listening to it— wishing it away." I propped myself up on one elbow and tried to stare into his face. A beard, eyebrows, and expressionless eyes were all that peered out from his wool hat and a sleeping-bag hood.

"Craig, you look like a terrorist."

"Guess that makes you my hostage. Have you looked outside?"

"I don't even want to think about it. . . . Listen to that wind will you?"

Craig grunted as he wriggled into a sitting position and then squirmed around to crack the tent door enough to stick his head outside. Snow swirled into the tent, pushing past Craig as he struggled to see. "I can't see a damned thing, but it does seem brighter. I wonder if the others are up, too."

"Robert and Win would have visited our tent by now if we were going anywhere. Looks like another shitty day in paradise."

Craig zipped the tent door shut and flopped back onto his sleeping bag with a groan. "I just want this weather to lift so we can get off this damn mountain. I need to get off this mountain. I don't even frickin' care about summiting anymore!"

"Now, Craig, don't hold back. Why don't you tell us how you really feel?"

As miserable as we felt at this moment, to me, the summit offered essential meaning to our effort. Without the summit, what we had experienced and were experiencing now would be nothing more than an exercise in futility. I sat up and stared intently at Craig.

"You and I are both going to be glad we summited—it's the only worthwhile thing to come of all this! If we don't at least try for the summit, then this investment of time and a part of our lives will have been wasted."

As I spoke, I felt my own spirits being lifted. In trying to energize Craig, I was pumping life back into my own soul.

"We can and will do this!" The notion that I was fooling myself and Craig echoed in the darkest corners of my mind. "I'm going over to the medical tent to see what I can find out."

The medical tent. That was rich. Although a code of silence cloaked the accidents in a safe haven of mystery, it was becoming quite the morbid joke around camp that the only reason to head to the medical tent was to check the latest weather and get an update on the "B.C." (body count). Like the weather, that seemed to be changing daily.

As I wrestled with my thoughts on the inside, I wrestled

with my Gore-Tex parka and pants on the outside. Stiff from the cold, the suit felt as though it were made of cardboard. Ice crystals showered down around me as I grimaced and shoved myself into the "armor." My parka was no better. Frost gilded the outer fabric while the inner lining felt like a wet towel— now soggy from having rested across my sleeping bag as I battled to stay warm. Even my hood was a damp mess since I had positioned it so it covered my face while I slept. My reward for sleeping warmer was a parka hood soaked from the condensation caused by my breath. I suppose I could try to stop breathing.

In the greater scheme of things, none of this mattered. At least, that is what I kept trying to tell myself. All that really mattered was life and death. After all that we had been through and all that was sure to come, would any of us really have sufficient strength to see us to the summit? And, if we did try for the summit, would it be a smart move or just a sacrifice of pawns in a deadly game of chess?

I crawled outside and stretched my cramped limbs. Conditions, though still relatively wild, were perceptibly improved compared to the hell we had been enduring. I found irony in the knowledge that, on any previous climb, I would have remained huddled in the tent, believing these winds far too formidable to venture forth. Denali had apparently desensitized me, blinded me, or both. As I peered about, I could see Mount Foraker between gusts as it peeked out above the dense gray carpet of clouds below us. As if launched from the main group for attack missions, huge battleship-sized cumulus clouds rolled in and out, slamming again and again into the walls around us and then recoiling for yet another massive assault. It was like watching a movie in accelerated time-lapse photography. One moment the weather appeared to be lifting, then worsening, then lifting. My mood soared and crashed with each change.

Though all around us the weather appeared uncertain of which way to turn, our little camp sat under a clear patch of sky. As I wandered toward the medical tent, I saw Win, his Gore-Tex parka and suit hanging on him like a hand-me-down on a refugee. I watched him pace back and forth, staring one minute at the sky, then the camp, then at nothing as if lost in thought. If he was thinking what I was thinking, he was angry, frustrated, and definitely itching to move, climb, anything but stay here or retreat. We had been sitting on this lousy little ice shelf at 14,000 feet getting the crap pounded out of us for too long to quit. When the time came, I would be willing to leave the mountain battered, but definitely not defeated. If it were up to me, there was only one way to go now and that was up.

But it wasn't up to me, so I hurried over toward Win and positioned myself so that he would have to pass by me as he paced. As Win approached, arms crossed, my words almost surged out of my mouth on a mission of their own, but I managed to reign them in before they spewed forth. Seeking answers to the uncertainties that were burning a hole in my gut would only create more tension.

Instead of a verbal assault, I managed a rather cool and reserved, "What do you make of it?"

Win stopped and stood next to me, staring at the sky with no expression showing on his sparsely bearded face. His usual animation and wit were apparently on vacation during this morning of uncertainty.

"It's hard to say, Ruth Anne. Robert has been on the radio all morning trying to get information. You can't trust the forecasts, though. One minute it looks better, the next, worse." Win spoke as though he were speaking to himself, although I knew he was speaking to me. Sandwiched as we were between the clouds below, the clouds above, and those swirling masses that kept hurling themselves at the walls around us, this was a decision that would haunt any leader. Make the wrong call, and we might all die.

Win shook his head and then walked past me to continue his pacing. "We're just going to have to wait for now and see how things develop over the next few hours," he called over his shoulder, apparently to no one in particular.

Finding no comfort in Win's words, I strode off to the medical tent but found it abandoned by all. No people, no sign, no nothing—other than the body bags. I headed back. I began clearing the night's accumulation of snow from around the tent and then entertained myself by chipping a layer of ice, several inches thick, from under the tent's rain fly. Hours passed as Craig and I watched the changeable sky and tried to second-guess Mother Nature. By noon, the conditions remained unstable with no shift in sight.

A stone's throw away, Robert had paced back and forth all morning, neck craned, and cuddling the radio like an infant to keep it warm and working. He looked at no one, intent upon his own analysis of the situation, and none of us dared approach him. Robert shouldered well the responsibility of being the leader, knowing all eyes were studying his face for unstated messages, a telling gesture, a break in composure, a crack in his veneer. His will was a force of nature.

We watched as if observing an ancient ritual. Instead of a holy robe, Robert wore a red parka covered with expedition patches (the 1984 American Everest Expedition, the 1987 Snowbird Everest Expedition, the 1990 Everest International Peace Climb, to name a few), a testament to his experience on world-class peaks. All that experience had to come into play in this one decision—up or down. Finally, this mountain priest ceased pacing, looked toward us and then strode purposefully in our direction. Pulses quickened.

"What's the call, Robert?" I asked.

"It's a hard one for sure. There are conflicting reports, but nothing that means a damn. Reminds me of '86. We were here at 14,000 feet, had been hit with a storm that broke up and looked just like it does now. Later that day, it sucked in a high-pressure ridge and things improved. I have a feeling it's going to do that here. I'm going to go with my gut."

I trusted Robert. "If you say up, then I am 100 percent behind that call," I said to him. I could only hope he was right.

"Thanks, Ruth Anne. Regardless, we have to retrieve our supplies, as we can't advance or retreat safely without them. Let's pack up and move everything with us, hedging a bet that, by the time we reach 16,500 feet and our food cache, conditions will improve. If it gets worse, we'll come back down and get the hell off the mountain. If not, we'll be positioned to move on to the high camp at 17,200 feet and a shot at the summit. Sound okay to you?"

"Yesssss!" I exploded. "We're really going up!"

Robert's teeth flashed in a broad grin. "Let's get everyone loaded up and move."

Prancing off, I chortled, "We're going for it. We're really *going to do it*!"

As we started packing for the assault, Craig grinned and chimed in, "Anything beats spending another night here!"

Mountaineering is rooted in extreme risk, and playing the odds becomes part of the game. With our food and fuel now exhausted, we had no choice but to go after our reserves. The climb up the headwall would take hours but, with a little luck, we could reach the cache without incident. Taking our camp with us would offer additional protection if we found ourselves in a situation from which we couldn't flee. If conditions improved, as Robert felt they might, the long hours of daylight would enable us to proceed to high camp. If not, we would have to camp on the knife edge of a violently exposed ridge or attempt to turn back. Getting a shot at the summit was a calculated gamble, but it was a bet all of us were hoping to win.

Still, even though this was our last shot at the summit, we would not fall prey to "summit fever"—a reckless abandon calling for reaching the top at any cost. We had made the right moves so far. Robert and Win were not about to ruin the record or risk our lives or their own with a rash decision. It was one step at a time, and this next step led toward the cache and survival.

Thwup-thwup-thwup announced the arrival of a single helicopter as we began breaking down camp in earnest. The sound was a grim reminder of the cost of gambles lost. The only reason that helicopter was landing was to pick up the body bags and shuttle them down the mountain. It would be an end to the saga of fatalities, we hoped.

The team mobilized quickly, freeing tents sunken into the ice and frozen in place. It wasn't until I collapsed ours, scraping off the remaining buildup of frozen snow, that a discovery sent a sharp pain of fear stabbing into my gut. A spiderweb pattern of wear marks, through which daylight could be clearly seen, covered the surface of our tent. It had been brand-new when we began the climb. Now the fabric looked as though it had been tied in knots and dragged repeatedly across rocks and concrete.

My God, I thought. One sharp tug could tear our fragile home in two. Our only shield against nature's wrath was on the verge of destruction. I stuffed the nylon shell gingerly into its sack and chose not to mention it to Craig.

Being absorbed in packing, it took me quite a while to notice the climbers from other teams gathering silently to watch us. Most of these faces observing our ritual were new, the others having departed the mountain by foot or body bag. Vacant faces surrounded us, their eyes masked in goggles and black-lensed mountaineering glasses. We had been on the mountain longer than anyone, and these faces knew that. I knew that they had heard what we had suffered and that we were low on food. I also knew that their silent gazes carried an element of hope. If we made it to 17,200 feet, ours would be the first team to survive the effort this season, paving the way to the summit for everyone. And to summit after surviving the storm would be an off-the-chart achievement.

With camp finally dismantled, we were ready to load up.

My crampons, the metal claws for navigating over glare ice, were strapped to the bottom of my climbing boots. I tromped about, tightening them after every few steps until they felt just right. To lose a crampon here could mean death. After one last check, I stepped into my climbing harness, the nylon belted sling that would act as a safety net should I tumble. Even with all the layers of clothing, I could barely cinch it up enough to keep it from slipping off my emaciated waist. The hardware hanging from the harness weighted it down further—carabiners, ascenders, and a pulley—tools for performing a one-woman rescue operation should the need arise, or for assisting with my own rescue, if I was conscious and able.

We uncoiled two climbing ropes and tied off knotted loops at 25-foot intervals, marking each climber's position on that line. Clipping one loop into a carabiner centered on the front of my harness, I took my place along our umbilical cord, tethering us together and binding our shared fate. Jack, Craig, and John did likewise behind me. Each rope team would have five climbers, the first led by Robert, the second by Win.

Having taken our stations on the rope, we stood ready, all our worldly possessions heaped upon our backs. We waited while Win and Robert performed a final sweep of camp to make sure nothing vital had been left behind.

Robert heaved his huge pack, easily half the size of his body, onto his back and clipped in ahead of me. Looking back at me with a tense smile, he said, "This is it—you ready?"

I was practically tugging at the rope like a sled dog who hasn't been allowed to run in weeks. "Ready? I've never been more ready!"

"Let's move, then."

More faces came out of their tents nearby to join those who had been silently watching us all this time. They formed a line to bid us good luck and farewell. There was an element of finality to their gesture that made my stomach knot up and popped a lump into my throat. My emotional armor that I had worked so hard to keep in place was beginning to crumble.

I felt an almost overwhelming desire to run over and hug each one of them, but I stared straight ahead, unable to return their gazes and smiles without cracking under the weight. I focused instead on our immediate objective, the 2,000-foot headwall.

Robert moved forward, setting the pace, as our two ropes snaked through camp. From here on, the serious and difficult climbing would begin, up the rock cliffs to the most famous landmarks in American mountaineering—names that for a climber raise the gooseflesh, haunt nightmares, and fuel imaginations—the West Buttress, Denali Pass, the Archdeacon's Tower, and the South Peak.

Our muscles were withered, unused to climbing after ten days in tents. My arms and legs felt heavy and, at times, useless. I leaned on my ice ax to help support my body, burdened by the 60-pound pack. Bent forward into the wind, I found it difficult to hold my head up. I became engrossed in the wind ridges carved in the snow below me, like sand dunes drifting before a storm. The climbing was agonizing, unrelenting, and my mind scrambled desperately for a way out. *Put everything out of your mind and climb. Don't push yourself. Relax, go slowly, pressure-*

breathe, I kept silently repeating. I made myself inhale deeply then exhale forcefully every couple of steps.

I had learned how to work through pain and fatigue thresholds. Lacking the brute strength and youth of other climbers, I conserved energy by meditating on the word *relax* and trying to ease every muscle in my body with each exhaled breath. Zen climbing—focus on the objective, not the distance. Unconscious effort. Once you get there, you will know it. What I have learned over the years is that true strength is not found in muscle bulk or size.

Occasionally, I was able to look up. Almost two weeks after the storm had hit, the last of the clouds were lifting. We climbed all afternoon to the accompanying drone of airplanes and the *thwup-thwup* of helicopters searching for the snow-covered remains of the Korean party. With each step, we were leaving the lurid scene of body bags and pressing higher toward the light.

It was five P.M. when we reached our cache at 16,500 feet. Although the temperatures continued to dictate wearing expedition parkas, the winds had subsided, the skies had cleared. Robert had called it right!

We decided to push on to the high camp, another 700 feet up the narrow West Buttress Ridge. In places, the more difficult maneuvers required hand-over-hand climbing made all the more challenging by the weight of our heavy packs. Exposure inched up the pucker factor as sphincters tightened and lips grimaced. As our team worked its tenuous way up the rock spine, glare ice and snow dropped away precipitously on either side. With each step, a tiny prayer was offered to the mountain gods to help the crampon points gain solid purchase. Even though my metal points were not penetrating, they managed to hold, leaving me feeling like a fly clinging to a featureless wall. One careless stumble to our left and the team would plunge 1,000 feet into a field of gaping crevasses. An untimely slip or a single gust of wind might catch us unawares and could send us tumbling to the right on a gruesome one-way journey down 2,000- to 3,000-foot walls with no hope of return—a fate that had already claimed five lives during the storm. Of course, it wasn't the fall that bothered me so much as the landing.

The rope tugged yet again behind me and I tensed myself for an impending fall, ready to drive my ice ax into the snow in the hope of arresting the fall and saving myself and all who were on the rope behind me. Fortunately, it was just Jack, who was moving so slowly that he was beginning to lag, causing the rope length between us to tighten and release with irritating frequency. I shot Jack a look, but it was clear that his only problem was fatigue. He was bent over, moving stiffly and erratically. Jack's inability to keep up and hold his own was not only slowing the team down, it was creating a situation where he was sapping my strength with each yank and snap of the rope. None of us had any excess energy. Though it may sound cruel, I had enough to do getting just myself up the mountain without the added task of pulling Jack along, too. Worse, since we were unable to keep up a steady pace, the specter of hypothermia began to loom large as we could not go fast enough to ward off the penetrating cold.

Robert, who was ahead of me on the rope, kept looking back, his expression and body language inquiring about the problem.

All I could do was shrug, turn around, and attempt to signal our "deadweight" to pick up the pace. This became too much for Jack, who eventually let his feelings become abundantly clear with a single, explosive *"Fuck you!"*

The knife ridge eventually tapered downward, leveling into a vast dish-shaped area, the high camp at 17,200 feet. To the east towered a 2,000-foot granite spire with walls so vertical that they remained free of snow, a stark contrast to the white world surrounding it. Below this monolith, the glacier continued up a steep, 1,000-foot windswept pitch leading to Denali Pass and on toward the summit.

To our right, the bowl spilled into a 3,000-foot vertical chute, the fast and lethal way back to the ice shelf at 14,000 feet. From this dizzying perch, we could view Mount Foraker and the Kahiltna Glacier extending back to our early camp at 8,000 feet. Tiny specs of color, tents perched on the ice shelf below, our frozen home for the last ten days, were the only evidence that others were clinging to this mountain as well. It was humbling to realize just how tiny we all were on this jumble of rock and ice—tiny ants clinging to a world that was not our own.

It was now eight P.M. We had climbed 3,200 vertical feet in one day following ten days in captivity. Although we were the first to be freed from the grip of the storm and the first team to reach this altitude on Denali this year, we were far from free. The snail's pace had taken a toll, leaving me, Franklin, John, and Paul somewhat hypothermic and in need of warmth and recovery. After quickly throwing up a tent, taking care not to shred the already rice-paper-thin fabric, we took turns warming ourselves inside while the others began building camp. It didn't take long for the shivering to stop—perhaps adrenaline, perhaps a need to be busy—and we were soon outside with the rest of our team, racing to beat the sun before it sank low on the horizon, out of sight for the time being behind distant peaks, sending the temperatures plummeting below the minus-20-degrees Fahrenheit mark where they now hovered.

While everyone was busy, Robert pulled me aside. His eyes probed mine as he quietly and patiently asked, "Ruth Anne, what was going on behind me on the rope today?"

"I think Jack was pretty beat, and I can't keep dragging him up the mountain. Every time I tried to take a step forward, the rope went tight yanking me backward. I can't keep that up. I even chilled enough to feel hypothermic for the first time on this mountain—really saps your energy."

Robert nodded, "I hear you. . . . I'll put him behind me tomorrow. That should straighten things out."

"Thanks Robert." I was more grateful than he could have known. If I had to go one more day tugging Jack along behind me, I was not sure that I would have the strength to continue.

Franklin once again proved his prowess and engineering skills as he led the way in constructing our new camp. I imagine that, given enough time, he could have fashioned high-rises out of ice. Bundled in a down expedition parka and topped with a knit hat, his thickly bearded six-foot-three frame seemed massive, almost Paul Bunyan–ish. All that was missing was his pet cow, Blue. His boundless energy and strength here at high camp were more amazing considering that only just last year, he had had to be evacuated after succumbing to altitude sickness.

"I am amazed at how strong you still are, Franklin," I marveled.

The ice mason paused long enough to breathe deeply and grin. "Failure can be a great motivator. If the same thing had hit me this year on the mountain, I wouldn't have been able to retreat." Franklin took a deep breath and stopped smiling—his eyes squinting under the glare of a distasteful thought. "And, who knows? I could have ended up like that Swiss guide, another stiff in a body bag waiting for a ride back home."

I nodded solemnly as Franklin turned back to the task at hand. There was no denying that we now occupied the elevation range known to climbers as the "death zone," where the effects of altitude are compounded, ravaging stamina and youth with lightning speed. The body's cells no longer regenerate themselves. Tissues, membranes, and capillaries deteriorate. Fat can no longer be digested or stored. To compensate, the body looks to use fat stored in the muscles, ultimately consuming the muscles themselves. In short, at this altitude and above, climbers literally begin digesting themselves—involuntary cannibalism. At these altitudes, calories cannot be taken in fast enough to maintain body weight, and it is a medical fact that a prolonged stay will lead to death.

The objective is to remain only long enough to get the job done and get safely off the mountain. At such elevations, strength collides with the destructive nature of extreme altitude. Climbers know they will be physically weaker, move more slowly, and fatigue more rapidly. Too often, they put themselves right on the edge when they go for the summit, reaching it cold, dehydrated, and exhausted. Most of them are lucky, most of the time.

Mental functions are also impaired. Oxygen starvation can cloud judgment, making formidable hurdles of even the most rudimentary matters. Bradford Washington, the first to summit Denali, estimated that within the death zone on Denali, a person is reduced to 50 percent of mental capacity, and not always aware of it, either. A common joke among alpinists is that to climb, one must be "brain-dead" which, to an extent, is true. It might also qualify as a prerequisite for the sport.

Later that evening, while resting in our tent, Craig's whisper cut through the quiet with an intensity that spoke to fear and uncertainty. "Ruth Anne, my head is throbbing. I can't rest. Do you have a headache, too?"

While having a headache on the mountain at this altitude is no reason for panic, Craig's alarm concerned me even though it was justified. He was on the edge, fighting for control. The headache was just a symptom and the underlying reason for a potentially bigger problem—panic. The haunting notion of the Swiss guide dying without possibility of evacuation was weighing heavily on his mind for sure. I knew I had to calm him down and fast. He had worked so hard to get to this point and had been so great on the mountain. The last thing I wanted to see was him blowing up and missing the shot at success on the summit, a success he richly deserved.

Trying to put on a calm face and a smile, I teased Craig. "Hey, no brain, no headache. . . . Consider your headache a credit to your intellect and the fact that you are just more cerebral than I am."

Not even a glimmer of a smile—he was in deep. "God, I

can't believe elevation is affecting me, after all this time on the mountain. You would think I would have acclimatized by now!"

"Look, Craig...don't be so hard on yourself. We had a brutally hard day and that is all there is to it. You are expecting too much of yourself. Remember that you have never been this high before on any mountain—altitude is serious stuff. Until you reach an elevation, you never know how hard it will hit you and there is no way to predict whether or not you will be affected. It's not a matter of strength, either. Just because I don't feel it now, doesn't mean I won't feel it tomorrow, or the next day or even the next—you never know!"

I was relieved at my own proven tolerance for altitude, especially considering all that we had endured. I had been to 23,000 feet on Aconcagua without incident, either, but as I spoke to Craig, my own words rang hollow—there are no guarantees. Even Sir Edmund Hillary, who first summited Everest, was later carried off another mountain at only 20,000 feet with pulmonary edema.

Craig pursed his lips tightly and gazed intently at me. "Jesus, Ruth Anne. I'm really worried I could get cerebral edema. This headache could be just the beginning."

This was getting out of hand. "Craig! You won't get it... trust me. Here's an aspirin. Drink plenty of water. Pressure-breathe, hard. It'll help."

I breathed with him for half an hour, in and out, in and out, forcefully expelling the air before gulping down another breath. We breathed together and he calmed down. The aspirin began to take effect. Taking no chances, I made him drink some of my water in addition to his own. I could top off before morning.

As Craig worked out his personal crisis, I told him about the medical article our doctor on Aconcagua brought along to shock us titled, "Mental Retardation Caused by Extreme Elevation." A smile worked its way along Craig's lips. Before long, we were amusing ourselves by discussing our possible mental damage from mountaineering. Clearly we were products of our sport.

Following what we deemed to be our "last supper," we flopped back into our bags and lay awake, tucked inside our tents waiting and praying for favorable conditions to make our summit bid. Tomorrow would be a new day, but would it be the kind of day we needed? As my breath ebbed and flowed from my lungs, it occurred to me that here, on this snowy shelf at high camp, we were but specks of flesh and bone clinging to an almost unfathomable enormity of rock, ice, and snow. We were the only living beings who dared tread in the death zone—where life is fleeting and every minute spent is a minute too long. We were on the threshold and had passed that critical point of no return where it was farther to retreat than to go forward.

SATURDAY, MAY 23
Day twenty-one on the mountain

We were down to the last of our food. We had no more chances left to try for the summit. I pried open my eyes to the sound of Craig unzipping the tent door only to have them slammed shut again by the intensity of the sunlight that flooded through the tent walls. We had awakened to our first totally clear day in three weeks, but still the wind howled.

"What do you make of it?"

"The sky looks good, but it's awful windy. I sure don't want to get caught up higher in anything more serious than sunshine, and wind, as we've learned, usually means weather. There's no telling what we'll do. That's Robert's and Win's call. It's really cold, that's for sure." With that weather report, Craig quickly closed the door and burrowed back into the warmth of his sleeping bag.

The high-pressure system had brought with it a drop in temperature and the thermometer hovered at a cutting minus-40 degrees Farenheit. Exposed to the teeth of the wind, the air felt so cold that we couldn't even manage to stand still long enough to eat breakfast. I donned goggles and face protection just to move about camp, and the others quickly followed suit. As I breathed, I could feel my breath condensing and then freezing solidly against the inside of my face mask. Peering out behind face masks and from under hoods, our high-tech-garbed group looked like raiding marauders from a *Star Wars* movie.

The day was brilliant and bitter without a cloud in sight. Snow plumes gyrated into the air at regular intervals, swirling like whirling dervishes leaving a trail of shimmering snow— fairy dust—suspended across the sky until the next 40-mile-per-hour rush of wind swept the slate clean and started the snow swirling again. It was the best start to a day we had seen since arriving on the mountain twenty-one days earlier.

Robert and Win made the call to go for it. This was it: Judgment Day. The moment of truth had arrived. The pain and suffering of the prior three weeks were all bundled up in this one attempt at success. We would attempt the summit, but not blindly. Always, in our back pocket, we would reserve the option of a safe retreat. No one spoke about the possibility for disaster, only the inevitability of success. If the blue skies above would only hold.

Ahead of us lay 3,000 feet to the summit. Once there, we would turn around and return to this camp for the night, a round-trip of 6,000 arduous feet in one day. We loaded our packs, each with a half gallon of water, a few candy bars, and extra warm clothes, and then we roped up. Robert led our team, with Jack now positioned directly behind him as promised, myself, then Craig and John. Vern, Paul, John, and Franklin were tied into Win on the second rope. At eleven-thirty A.M. our procession filed out of camp toward Denali Pass.

Our actions were slow and robotic as we crept up the steep wall above camp. The wind and thin, cold air were debilitating, the climbing extreme. We down-shifted, taking two breaths per step. Each step was now a deliberate process—lock the back knee and rest, exhale twice and take one more step forward, lock the back knee and rest, breathe, breathe, take one more step forward, lock the back knee . . . breathe, breathe, step, try to enjoy the mountain, the moment. Take in the light. Stay centered, stay focused. Relax, relax . . . pacing myself, the word *relax* again became my mantra for the day.

The slow, rhythmic gait was hypnotic. Mesmerizing. Climbing, I became lost in the windswept snow at my feet.

This is good, I thought. We are part of a great event here.

Soon, I no longer heard myself breathing. The wind filled my head, preventing ordered thoughts and triggering responses at a primal level—moving and reacting to the elements to ensure survival. The mindless journey.

Though the Alaska sun never sets in May, it had been totally obscured behind a murky sky for weeks. After dwelling in a world devoid of color or life, we now found ourselves blinded by a brilliant white light radiating from every direction. We traversed fields of sparkling snow, sculpted by hurricane-force winds—a moonscape of space and emptiness in a timeless Arctic wilderness.

We pressed onward. Occasionally I'd hear Robert blast Jack in front of me, yelling at him to keep moving. The pace was good. My altimeter registered 19,000 feet. As the air thinned further, we began to gulp down three breaths for each step. Breathe, breathe, breathe, step, plant the ice ax, lock the knee. Even in the frigid temperatures, my body was dripping with sweat from the effort. We were all willing participants in a slow-motion marathon, pushing against a brick wall: altitude.

Every hour we took a ten-minute rest break. We'd grab a drink of water, a bite of a candy bar, adjust equipment, and deal with bodily needs. It was too cold to stay any longer than that. We had to keep moving to prevent our muscles from stiffening. Floating like a dark thought in the back rooms of my mind was the notion that more than one climber has sat down, become drowsy from fatigue, freezing temperatures, and lack of oxygen, closed his eyes, and never stood up again.

We halted below Archdeacon's Tower, a prow of granite jutting 19,650 feet into the sky. The second rope team struggled up behind us. Vern was gasping and moaning, fighting with every ounce of energy he had to complete each step, each breath. I winced as I watched him labor up the mountain behind us. Vern was planting his ice ax in front of him—leaning on it with both hands, his head hanging with exhaustion between his arms, his eyes staring at his feet, his mouth gaping wide open. He used each laborious thrust of his ice ax as a means of leverage to drag his spent body up the mountain's face. Upon reaching the Tower, Vern collapsed with relief at our feet. It hurt to watch him struggle so, but at the same time I had to admire his effort.

Between labored gasps in the rarefied air, Vern peered out from frosted, wire-rimmed glasses and moaned to anyone who was listening, "I . . . don't . . . know . . . if . . . I'm . . . going . . . to make . . . it." His voice was raspy from the cold and the sheer effort required just to breathe.

"Sure you are," Win replied firmly. "Stop talking and have a drink. We are all going to make it!"

Vern's self-doubt at this point was understandable and his feelings were probably shared by others in our group, but no one had admitted it. I would imagine that, for some, verbalizing the pain and fatigue they felt could make the feelings that much more real and spiral them into a world of defeat.

Step by step we worked our way across glacier fields, riddled by crevasses, traversed rock and ice ridges, and pushed forward up gleaming blue walls of ice. The weather continued to hold and the sun beat down mercilessly upon us. To make breathing easier, we had all pulled off our face masks, leaving our skin exposed to both the intensity of high-altitude ultraviolet rays and the extreme cold. It was like walking on a treadmill positioned directly under a bank of heat lamps, except you couldn't feel the heat, you just knew it was there, burning your skin without feeling. Windburn, sunburn, freezing flesh—if it wasn't one thing, it was another. I was almost afraid to smile for fear part of my face might crack off.

We climbed upward inexorably for seven hours. We walked to a rhythm of a song that never changed—step, plant, lock, breathe, breathe, breathe, step, plant, lock, breathe, breathe, breathe. . . . By six in the evening, our cluster of mountaineering automatons had reached "the football field," a shallow one-mile-square concavity in the frozen terrain. The winds had ceased, as though by magic, and our shadows lengthened across the snow. Everywhere, the light had become less harsh, softening as the sun descended in the sky. We dropped our packs to rest and regroup our thoughts and energy before making the final push to the summit ahead. From where we rested, the glacier swept up a smooth and virtually featureless 500-foot pitch, ending in the summit ridge—the object of my desires these last twenty-one days.

For the first time, our dream of reaching the summit was tangible. I could actually see the thing I had lived for in my imagination. Set in stark contrast to the blue-black sky, the gleaming knife ridge crested at the South Peak, the 20,320-foot summit of Denali. Now, with the end so near and in sight, my body felt flush with a renewed sense of energy. It was premature to revel in a victory still to come, but it was also hard not to feel an almost overwhelming sense of accomplishment and pride.

"How are you feeling, Vern?" Robert asked.

"I'll make it. . . ." replied Vern almost breathlessly, his voice still raspy from the effort of getting to this point. "I've always believed . . . I could just pedal harder . . . find another gear . . . no matter how hard or how steep . . . Guess it doesn't work that way."

"Hey, you'll find the gear you need to get you to the top. Count on it. Most of us are like mountain bikes carrying gears around we've never used ... Well, now you get to shift down and use them."

"You know, the summit still seems an awful long way away," sighed Paul, his thick black beard glistening with ice.

"Climbing and summiting are two entirely different things," I mused as I gazed toward the summit. There is no way you can ever equate the destination with the journey. Both are important, but both are also different.

"Nothing worthwhile is easy, Ruth Anne. You don't have to be the best climber in the world or the one who makes the summit to be appreciated for the effort."

"That's true, Paul, but just the same, I have been with people who've never actually left basecamp yet still claimed the mountain's summit as their own."

"You know someone who actually did that?" Paul was incredulous.

"Yes. After all, mountains don't talk and no one is the wiser. This is, after all, a sport without many witnesses."

"Yeah, maybe, but to lie ..." his voice drifted off, his gaze fixed on the mountain.

"Sure changes your feelings about putting your life on the line with a person when you know something like that about them. Still, that's not going to happen here. We're all going to the summit!"

Robert passed around hard candy to suck on. We were running on fumes at this point and any source of energy was welcome as there was still plenty of hard work ahead. We drank deeply and the icy shock made our stomachs cramp and heads split—nine times worse than a summer day's ice-cream head-

ache. Paul spilled a little as it sloshed around his lips. The drop-
lets froze in midair, like a scene from a Jack London story, and
shattered as they hit his boot. I was definitely impressed by the
intensity and power of the cold.

We gratefully left our packs and forged ahead, unburdened
as we moved up the smooth wall of virgin snow leading to the
summit ridge. A dead calm had fallen over the mountain like a
veil. Only our labored breathing and the clanging of metal hardware could be heard, and even those were quickly muffled by
the depth of the snow and the silence of the mountain.

Ice crystals glittered like tiny diamonds on the ground in
front of me. I felt light and buoyant—better than during any
previous final ascent. We were lucky. Everyone was hanging
tough, and the mountain was finally cooperating. However, the
battle isn't over until the hill is won, and we were still a good
distance from our ultimate goal. Anything could happen between
here and there.

When we reached the crest of the 500-foot pitch, we turned
our backs to the sun to follow the knife's edge of the ridge on
up to the top. There it was—the top of the continent—in full
view, within our reach. Before us, a half mile of gradual climbing on the sharp edge of a colossal rock fin was all that separated
us from the ice cap crowning the summit. We were within striking distance. I could hardly believe it, after all that we had been
through—we hadn't died, we had survived, we had been strong
enough to match the mountain. Our survival had been a
choice—the right choice.

It was almost too good to be true. I glanced over my shoulder, looking for a storm cloud or any one of a dozen imagined

nemeses that might be lurking to foil our efforts. There was no storm, no devilish trick or specter of bad fortune, only the dazzling white Arctic sun that hung in the sky, just as it had every day since time began, and would until time ended, with or without us there to watch it. Knowing this same sun was shining back home on those I loved was a bond—for me, a sharing of the moment with them. It was my sister's birthday.

The sharp points of my crampons dug into the ice and snow, scratching and creaking as we broke trail up the ridge. Everyone was holding steady. Jack, still ahead of me on the rope, was climbing well, holding the pace and moving smoothly. After hours of prodigious effort, the team moved in unison, like a well-oiled machine, surefooted and strong.

My thoughts and emotions welled to the surface and nearly spilled over in a powerful surge. "Yes! We are going to do it. . . ." I felt like dancing up the rest of the way. My dreams were being realized.

Here, in the most dramatic setting on earth, reality exceeded expectation. Off to our left, the glacier fanned down into an enormous snow field, pulled irresistibly toward the valley below by the forces of gravity. To our right, the ridge plunged precipitously 9,000 vertical feet to the glacier floor below in one of the single greatest drops on earth. Huge cornices formed by the gale-force winds clung precariously, overhanging the escarpment and waiting for a signal—a loud noise, a shaking of the earth, a mountaineer's misstep—to break loose and cascade in a massive shower of ice and snow. The perilous knife ridge, only a few feet wide, marked the convergence of these two faces. A wind blast, poor visibility, or an untimely stumble could send all of us free-falling in a tumbling, twirling mass of flesh and rope to the bottom, nearly two miles distant. A one-way ticket with no return privileges.

The drone of an airplane's engine broke through the muffled silence near the peak. Robert had radioed basecamp earlier to report our progress. The operator had relayed the news to Talkeetna, and a bush pilot flew in now to buzz the top, tipping his wings with each pass in a salute to our success. The aircraft was so close we could even see a camera mounted to the side of the cockpit. When we stepped to within one hundred yards of the summit, we paused, unable to collectively resist the urge to whoop and holler and wave our ice axes triumphantly in the air. I could only hope the pilot was getting this all on film. The plane circled and zoomed overhead for almost forty-five minutes until finally leaving to refuel. We had arrived.

The sun bathed the peak in evening light. We edged our way across the last undulation in the ridge, until finally there was nowhere higher to climb. At seven P.M., Robert reached the top, followed by Jack, myself, Craig, and John. The second team joined us moments later. A humble, awed, and respectful group stood clustered together atop the highest point in North America.

Relief. Such utter relief. It was as though the weight of the world had been lifted off my back. The emotions that I had pushed deep within myself for the sake of survival knotted up in a lump and rose to the back of my throat. I tried to swallow and will the lump away, but I could not. Although I felt elated, there was no way I was going to act out my thrill by running pell-mell about the summit. After all, the pinnacle we were perched on was so small there was no place to go but down, straight down.

There was no dishonesty with emotions on this summit. No false bravado. Tears flowed and froze on a number of cheeks. For myself, lump in the throat and all, I had no tears to shed. I was simply thrilled to be there. My thoughts drifted from the summit to everyone I loved—Bob, my family and friends, Peso. I was calm, peaceful, acutely aware of everything past and present and the interconnection of things—that nature is not something outside ourselves, but who we are. I marveled at what once seemed important, such as possessions, plans ... Here, high above the mayhem of the world, I found myself reminded that it's not how much we have, but how little we need, that counts.

The same mountain that earlier had unleashed such wrath now chose to reserve its choicest gift for those who had dared venture to the apex. We had found our Holy Grail and now drank deeply from the chalice. With not so much as a breath of wind to stir the air, the cloudless conditions afforded views in all directions, of hundreds of miles of ice, snow, melting glaciers, and tundra—the legacy of the past, frozen in time. If I squinted hard enough, I could almost imagine the edge of the world.

It is true that the mountain had taken—exacted a price from those who dared seek its prize—but now it willingly gave back. The power of the view from the top is the connection between what is tangible, seen and felt, and the knowledge gained by pushing the outer limits of our endurance. It's a power each assigns to a place by our response to it. For me, experiencing this moment was to realize God.

Everyone stood silently and pulled their frames a little taller than usual. Franklin, his beard decorated with a thick adornment of icicles, seemed to tower above the rest. He had risen from failure the previous year to a stunning success before enormous odds, and now was reaping the ultimate reward. We had all earned our place in one way or another. Although there is little doubt that not all of us could have made it without support of the team, there was no denying that every climber had reached the top under his own power, one foot in front of the other. Each had found his own strength in his own way.

For Robert and Win as well, the success was not only the summit, but in guiding us safely through a mental odyssey. Even more than the elements, the challenge had been ourselves.

Some places call to us for reasons unknown. We had traveled to a height few will ever attain. We had been drawn, against all odds, to come here and reach this summit. There had been no point or purpose other than the challenge itself. Some will ask why, but it is my feeling that the answer is not so important as the doing. The day we begin seeking a serious answer to the question is the day we will stop climbing mountains.

If there is an explanation, it may be simply this: that the value of wild places lies in showing us the way back—that wilderness is but a path back to the center of our souls.

There's something special in seeing a shared vision realized. Those for whom the struggle had been the greatest were now proudest of the accomplishment. We had become the products of our own imaginations in a lifetime event fulfilled. The Alaskan natives claim that God can be seen on Denali. For me, the mountain was God, and I would carry this moment forever.

Almost as suddenly as the silence had fallen over us, like a call to prayer, we snapped out of it and our little mountain congregation began to minister among ourselves.

"Ruth Anne, you were right the other day. The summit has made it all worthwhile." If Craig could smile any broader, the smile would have left his face. "I had no idea it would be like this. . . . And to think I just wanted off the mountain."

I nodded enthusiastically. "You helped me up this mountain, too, you know!"

"Good job, Ruth Anne," Robert said in his quiet way over my shoulder.

I turned to Robert, bursting with gratitude and a need to tell him how wonderful he was. "Thanks Robert. You're a great leader. One of the reasons I came on this climb was to have a chance to climb with you. I have never learned more!"

Win turned to me and smiled broadly, "Ruth Anne, I'll climb with you any time, any place in the world."

"Thanks Win. Coming from you, I take that as a real compliment. You did a great job of leading, too—a tribute to your family's storied mountaineering and guiding history."

And so it went, like a championship team in any sport reveling in the success and magic of the moment, kudos were passed around. If there had been champagne, and if it weren't so cold, and if we weren't so tired, the bubbly would have been flowing.

Paul, in his exuberance, blindsided me with a remark I wasn't used to hearing. "Ruth Anne, you are such a *stud*!"

I could only shake my head and laugh, every bit a woman, and yet still just one of the guys, I took the compliment in stride. "Thanks Paul, you do have such a special way with words."

Vern, who had battled every inch of the way to the summit, stood off to the side looking a little under the weather. Also not so focused on the celebration was Jack, who spent much of his time hopping around frantically trying to contain an attack of diarrhea. Reluctantly he finally approached me.

"Ruth Anne, did you pack along any toilet paper by chance?" he pleaded. It was quite the switch from the tone of voice that had screamed an obscenity at me only the night before. He was clearly on the verge of exploding.

I smiled, "Sorry, Jack, I chose not to summit with the toilet paper. It's down in my pack." What goes around comes around.

We took turns posing for pictures, balancing on the high point—a frozen outcropping, three feet square, jutting out from the ridge and suspended over the horrific 9,000-foot drop. The "one-wrong-step rule" applied as we coached one another not to venture backward while reveling in the glory of the moment.

"I'll take the first hundred copies!" Craig joked as I took his summit shot.

"And you deserve them," I answered.

My last act on the summit was to have Craig take a picture of me holding the Batton's Kids Climb capsule high in the air. Then, with a flick of my wrist, I launched the green capsule off the north side of the summit ridge—a side never visited, at least not on purpose, by other climbers. There, the capsule was sure to remain part of the mountain forever, fulfilling my promise to the Batton team leader.

After fighting for twenty-one days to reach this point, the team remained on top for only twenty minutes. Jack was definitely sick, and a number of others had developed "climber's cough." We sucked on hard candy, lemon drops, to help alleviate the pain and quiet the rasping and grating in our throats that we felt with each deep breath. To begin a spasm of uncontrolled coughing up here could literally rip our lungs apart and lead to sudden pulmonary edema and death. At such elevations, where the atmosphere contains less than half the oxygen available at sea level, the body becomes increasingly more fragile and subject to rapid deterioration. A short stay and a fast descent minimizes, though it doesn't prevent, the damage.

There's a mountaineering expression—"Once you reach the top, you're only halfway there." Covering the 3,000 feet from high camp to the summit had consumed seven hours and now would take another three to return. With the endless Alaska days providing light well into the night, we arrived safely back at 17,200 feet at ten-thirty P.M., just as the last rays of sun pulled back over the ridge, leaving only shadows behind.

High camp never looked so good. We crawled into our tents exhausted and barely able to talk between coughing seizures that racked our bodies and caused our brains to pound. As I removed my down expedition mittens, I discovered my thumbs had turned completely black. Despite insulating my ice ax with foam, my thumbs had rested against the bare metal shaft leaving an opening for frostbite to worm its way between the thick layers. I quickly tucked my hands up and under my down vest and next to my stomach until the numbness subsided. As with my feet, I hadn't felt the freezing, but would now have to suffer the pain of thawing. Still, there was a bright side—I was surviving just fine with black toes so there was no reason to think that black thumbs would be worse and, I observed somewhat darkly, at least my toes and thumbs matched!

As I sat there, cold thumbs pressed against my abdomen, it occurred to me that dying wasn't all that hard, but fighting to stay alive, coming back to life, that's what hurt.

Our summiting had been not just the conquering of a mountain. It had been a celebration of survival. We felt like undecorated heroes and rewarded ourselves at midnight with macaroni and cheese, practically the only food remaining in our stores. We had each climbed for the past twelve hours on subsistence rations consisting of a cup of oatmeal and a candy bar.

We sat quietly, downing our meal, reflecting on the mountain, and doing our best not to let coughing spasms ravage our lungs or send dinner spewing across the tent. Finally, after struggling, I had to put down my bowl.

"Craig, I can't finish eating. I don't think I have the energy left to digest a thing. You want it?"

"Thanks." He stared into his bowl, his lips pursed in contemplation. Then he whispered, "You know, I cried on top—thought I saw some of the others crying, too."

I nodded. Summiting had indeed been sweet. We'd called every move on this mountain to the wire and felt elated with our success. We had been allowed to peek at the mountain's treasure and felt blessed. The mountain, however, was not so impressed. Upon checking the radio for the weather report, Robert passed on the news—another storm was headed our way.

{10} THROUGH THE LOOKING GLASS

Day twenty-two on the mountain

I had slept the sleep of the dead, awakening in nearly the same position as when I lay down the night before. Exhaustion is a wonderful narcotic. This morning, however, I had no chance to luxuriate in the success of summiting or pamper the muscles that screamed for more rest after two days of heavy use. Urgency pressed me and the rest of the team into action. We had to beat the incoming storm down the mountain. Since technically we were out of food, Fig Newtons followed by a steaming hot apple-cider chaser served as breakfast. By nightfall, we hoped to be at 14,000 feet and then push on to Kahiltna Basecamp the following day. Though the end was in sight, it was a distant vision for a mind clouded with dusty cobwebs— so far, so little time, so tired.

Our team felt physically and mentally wasted. A few even stumbled around camp like common drunks. Paul had already stumbled, catching himself before actually falling, but cutting his hand on nearby rocks in the process. Then, he just stood there and watched the blood flow, fascinated by his own injury and unable to comprehend fully what had happened. The descent was going to be interesting. Most mountaineering accidents actually occur on the descent, the result of fatigue, mental letdown, or altitude sickness. While coming down from the summit of Aconcagua, one of our team not only failed to breathe properly, he sat down and refused to move. No one, not even Pete Whittaker, the team leader, could reason with him. He became irrational and cause for worry since climbers in this state have been known to become violent if others attempt to force them into something they don't want to do. After some coaxing, Pete managed to take his pack away from him and convince him that his brother should lead him by the hand back to camp. Once at camp, his senses returned to normal with little recollection of what had just transpired above. He became known from that moment on as "the first man to descend Aconcagua while holding his breath."

I was worried as we clipped into our ropes and began to head down. Minds were already off the mountain with talk of a celebration at the Fairview Bar in Talkeetna. Craig was talking of leading bike tours; I, of being on a schooner in Fiji with friends. This was not the time for distractions because it takes only a split second for the mountain to claim a soul as its own.

"Focus, goddammit! We're not off this thing yet." Robert's voice barked back at us. The team fell silent. No more babble, no more dreams of beers. Just step, step, step, step . . . Willing the mind to move the feet and watch where they are going.

Other teams began moving up the mountain toward High Camp. Our successful bid had opened the door to the summit and the climbing season was now officially open. Secretly I prayed no one else would die this summer and that the storm bearing down on us would carry only a fraction of the force of those preceding it. At this altitude, a mountaineer was at the mercy of a mountain. Denali, in particular, had shown little compassion for those who had attempted to scale her lofty heights so far this year.

As we worked our way down the fixed ropes at the headwall, a set of tent poles ricocheted past me, bouncing and sliding down the steep slope before disappearing into the same crevasse that had swallowed the Koreans almost a week ago.

"What in the hell was that?" Robert screamed up at us.

"Ahh, a set of tent poles from Vern's pack, I think," fired back Win from the head of the second rope team.

"You are kidding me. Were those our tent poles, Vern?" Robert clearly had had enough of Vern's bumbling and stumbling.

Vern launched into a breathless, panicked, and somewhat apologetic stream of consciousness: "Oh God . . . A strap must've worked its way loose or somethin'. . . . I mean, I don't know. . . . I know I tied the—it—they just worked their way loose an' . . . Oh man . . . now we don't have a tent and—"

"Oh, shut up, Vern!" Randy sounded as though he was ready to strangle him. He would have had to stand in line, though. We were all ready to strangle Vern.

"Calm down! Okay, we're going to finish the last section of fixed rope, work our way slowly over to the crevasse and then Win is going to belay me while I go down and retrieve the poles. Okay?" Robert firmly and confidently restored control to the near riot that was threatening to break out.

It was a worrisome decision to go after the poles, but there really was no choice. Our team was down one tent, which could put the entire team in jeopardy if a serious storm swept over us.

As we rested away from the edge of Jaws (the name the crevasse had previously earned for its gaping mouth and apparent hunger for human flesh), Robert and Win retrieved the poles—a dangerous task. Twenty nerve-racking minutes passed before Robert's head appeared over the edge with one hand held up triumphantly in the air, holding a pair of goggles.

"It's a gold mine of scattered gear down there. Got our poles and came back with a bonus prize of first-class goggles. Never would have found these if you hadn't lost the poles, Vern—thanks." Robert's voice carried an air of sarcasm.

Vern smiled sheepishly and mumbled something about being really sorry while we just continued glaring at him. Stupidity such as this deserved no early redemption.

"You gonna keep those goggles, Robert?" wondered Paul.

"Sure, why not?"

"Well, I mean, they might belong to one of the Koreans."

"Hey, they're not going to be needing them anymore now, are they?"

Paul fumbled a bit, clearly uncomfortable at the prospect of profiting from another's misfortune. "I guess not."

In my book, Robert needed new goggles. The Koreans didn't. They had lost theirs and, in reality, it was the mountain who had claimed them first. So in actual fact, it was the mountain rewarding Robert for risking his life for others. Seemed fair to me.

"Better make sure your brain is strapped in, okay, Vern? Wouldn't want you losing anything more," Randy chided as we headed out for the final short leg back into camp at 14,000 feet.

We burst out laughing. Vern remained stone-faced and silent.

The scene we walked into was a far cry from the one we had left. Ground blizzards with subzero temperatures and mountaineering camps huddling against the storm like sheep clustered before the slaughtering pen had been replaced by bright sunshine cascading down on a delightful scene of Technicolor tents surrounded by sunbathing climbers playing Nerf ball—a few even wore Hawaiian shirts. As we limped into camp on sore and frostbitten feet, we were surrounded by a bunch of enthusiastic, new, cleanly scrubbed faces, all equally amazed that we had been on the mountain for twenty-two days and had summited. They appeared as innocent cherubs next to our grizzled veteran, "we've survived the war" vestige of vacant eyes, sunken cheeks, raw and scabbed skin, and thick beards (other than on me, of course, although at this point, nothing would have surprised me). We became rock stars, living legends among a tiny cult of climbers. We had survived the storm and we had been to the promised land.

Not all were so easily impressed. While we had wanded off our ice-block encampment, indicating to all arriving climbers that another team occupied this spot and intended to return, we discovered it was now occupied by a European team whose leader had no intention of giving it up. They had even commandeered our dining cave. So much for supposed European class. So much for mountaineering etiquette.

Though the weather was clear and calm, we had to face the task of building ice-block walls before erecting our tents one last time. It was tempting to simply throw up our tents and crash, but experience had taught us that leaving anything to chance meant inviting disaster. Fortunately, members of other teams pitched in to help. Whether this was out of sympathy, or purely a good excuse to work shoulder-to-shoulder with someone who had summited and have the opportunity to talk with them, I didn't know. Whatever the reason, we were very grateful for the assist.

As we worked, one young climber mentioned that the crevasses down below were beginning to open and were getting quite frightening. Perfect!

Eager for more positive news, I edged toward another group and picked up the conversation somewhere in the middle. This man had been up on the West Ridge, the area where the Korean team had suffered their fatalities, and had actually seen the bodies. Mesmerized, I stopped working along with the rest of the crew to listen.

"I couldn't believe it. One of them, his skin was totally black from freezing. It was like he was mummified. His boot was missing, probably torn off during the screamer he took down the Express, and the crampons on his other boot were completely bent back. It must have been one nasty fall. Both his gloves were missing, too, although he might've had 'em off before the fall. His face is what got to me, though. Contorted into an agonized angle, it looked as though he'd screamed his entire way down and died mid-scream. His mouth was wide open, his eyes rolled back into his head. Man, it was eerie."

I shuddered as another in the group launched into a discussion about why so many Asians die on the mountain.

"One of the rescue pilots I saw at basecamp before we headed up was telling me that this had been the fourth time in six years he'd had to rescue Koreans from the mountain," one chimed in. "In fact, he said he'd rescued one guy twice, once in '86 and once in '88, from nearly the same spot."

"Go figure," said another. "Kinda makes you wonder, doesn't it. Why do they climb almost as if they have a kamikaze desire to succeed at any cost? Maybe it's the loss of face, the expense to get here, the pressure not to disappoint their sponsors or government. . . . Man, all I know is it's not worth it. The minute they start naming a famous chute 'the Canadian Express' is the day I stop climbing."

I turned, surmising that the man speaking must have been a member of a Canadian team trying to summit. Climbing this mountain is a high-profile event. It seems that the more people who die, the more attractive the challenge. Maybe that's what keeps the Koreans coming for glory—so many have died that those who make it are lionized. If that is true, it seems a high price to pay for the summit of a mountain that so many others from so many nations have climbed very safely. I knew in my heart that as a nationality, Koreans had no lock on apparent stupidity or mountaineering inexperience. Though statistics seem to back up the sweeping generalizations made around the world about the reckless disregard for safety and life that many Asian climbers exhibit, they are not alone. Climbers from every nation die in the mountains each year, more often than not from careless mistakes or reckless bravado.

Another Canadian, possibly a member of the same team as the one I had just heard speak, happened by and noticed, as I was positioning an ice block, that I had the same kind of boots as he did. He wondered if I could help him fix a pressure point. As I stopped work to help him perform surgery on his footwear, he saw fit to launch into a story—also about the Koreans. Morbid fascination had gripped the camp, pulling everyone into its grasp. Even though I didn't really want to hear it, I was a captive audience.

With wide eyes and an all-too-eager tremor in his voice, he began spinning his tale. "You know, I saw those three dead ones, the Koreans. Man, what a mess. Frozen blood and shit everywhere. They probably tumbled several thousand feet, all tangled together—like a giant inseparable ball of arms and legs. They fell into a crevasse at the bottom, one on top of the other, a mass of broken and twisted limbs held in place by Gore-Tex suits, and frozen together like a macabre piece of sculpture. Rescuers tried to pry 'em apart, but there was no way. So, they flagged in the helicopter and hooked them from a cable dangling from the bottom of the copter like a lump of meat at the meat market. I watched it fly off. A giant, brightly colored ball of frozen flesh swinging back and forth on its way to Talkeetna where they hoped to thaw the mess out and then bag and tag each body."

"Sounds ugly to me." It was a stupid comment, but all that I could manage as I handed back the lad his repaired boots.

"Yeah, it was more than ugly. It was completely gross. I couldn't stop staring. Hey, this fits great. Thanks."

And with that he headed off, leaving me to try and shake the grisly image of broken, mangled bodies dangling from a hoist. It was a scene I didn't want to relive, ever, but most certainly not here while I was still standing in the danger zone. I had to focus on life to ensure success.

As we were placing the last of the ice blocks and unloading the final sleeping bag into our tents, a member from a team from Boulder, Colorado, sauntered over and invited us to brunch. They had come this far but did not intend to climb any higher after hearing of the previous week's carnage and learning that another storm was on its way in. Their outing had amounted to nothing more than a strenuous picnic. Starving as we were, our group descended on theirs like a pack of locusts that had just sighted a farmer's precious stock of grain.

Denali park rules mandate that climbers depart the mountain with all their trash and any extra supplies, leaving nothing behind to despoil the pristine environment. Not wanting to lug their weighty gourmet pantry (the climber was dining on Brie, smoked oysters, and crackers when he wandered over with the invite), they were practically begging us to help them eat their way out of their predicament. Worse for them, they'd compounded their dilemma by caching food all the way down the mountain. Their invitation to meet the next day for sandwiches at 13,000 feet, dessert at 11,000 feet, and a mid-afternoon snack at 9,000 feet, was a long overdue streak of culinary fortune for us. None of us gave a moment's thought before accepting.

As I lay in our tent later that afternoon, soaking up the warmth and relaxing with no hunger pangs for the first time in weeks, my mind headed off on yet another quiet journey.

While in Tibet, several years earlier, a monk pressed a sacred amulet into my hand and then quickly disappeared into the crowd. Even though I knew Westerners were receiving religious icons from Tibetans as "gifts" to save them from destruction by the Chinese, I gave this occurrence no added thought. I even forgot to mention the gift to the Chinese customs officials, which was probably a good thing as it might have landed me in jail.

Two weeks after returning home, I wore the amulet while in San Francisco giving a presentation on Tibet. Shortly before my program, while browsing among the artifacts at an Asian art and antique store, an intense voice pierced through the mustiness.

"You've been to Tibet!" The words came from the direction of a tiny elderly Chinese gentleman who had been sitting behind a desk, but was now standing in shock, as though confronted by an apparition.

"Yes, but how'd you know that?"

He gestured. "Because of your amulet. You have a lama there."

"No. I don't know any lamas personally."

He peered toward me and insisted, "But you must or you would not have such a thing!"

"You misunderstand. This was given to me in a crowded place by a monk who then disappeared . . . I don't have any idea why."

"Ah ha! You see. You do have a lama. It was the monk. He chose you! Such amulets house sacred relics. Have you opened it?"

"Well, sure. It was tied shut by a string which had been there so long that it had left an impression in the metal—see?"

He looked and merely nodded. "And in it?"

"Just a peacock feather . . . would you like to see?"

He jumped back in horror, raising his arms before his face as if expecting a blow. "NO, NO, NO!" As he calmed, he whispered urgently, "You must not show this to anyone, it is for your eyes only. Only the Dalai Lama possessed such birds. He kept them at his summer palace in Norbulinga. Do you realize that by receiving this you have been blessed?"

I shrugged. I had heard this from others, but had always taken it as just a supreme compliment, not a meaning of any spiritual significance. An Apache woman had once told me I possessed "The Third Eye" and had invited me to share in sacred rituals seldom witnessed by outsiders.

"How did you know to wear it on black?"

"I don't know. It just seemed right, I guess. It seemed the only color appropriate."

"You must believe me, your life has been blessed. You have been chosen."

"I hope so," I replied, heading for the door, not sure what exactly had just transpired.

"Please, my name is David. Come see me whenever you are in San Francisco," he called urgently after me.

I began thinking of David and his store and his words and the amulet. I should visit him again. After all, considering the odds we had faced, certainly someone must have been watching over us.

Craig, slipping back into the tent, pulled me from my worldly travels.

"Have you heard? The storm. . . . It's a big one and it's expected to hit late tomorrow. Robert wants us up early and we're gonna race the wind to basecamp. If we make it, we'll most likely be in Talkeetna tomorrow night. If we don't, it's likely we'll be pinned down for days without food. Man, I just don't even wanna think about another few days in this shithole."

"Nor I. . . . We'll make it. I know it."

Now we'd see just how blessed I really was.

MONDAY, MAY 25
Day twenty-three on the mountain

The next storm loomed visibly on the horizon, a wave of pink-and-purple clouds stacked beautifully against the dark blue morning sky. It occurred to me that today was Memorial Day. May had been lost someplace in a blizzard. Camp was broken down in record time by impossibly beaten bodies driven by the need to leave this mountain, inspired to action simply by the thought of hot showers and cold beers just a plane ride away. All we had to do was hike to the runway, 14 miles distant and 7,000 feet below.

Though we were leaving, our loads felt almost as heavily weighted as when we had arrived, evidence of our weakened state. It was not a joyous expedition. Our sleds refused to follow obediently and were instead responding to gravity by lurching ahead of us, riding up the backs of our legs, rolling down side hills and tripping us. Now I understood why Robert and Win had suggested naming our sleds after someone we disliked, so we could vent our rage with conviction and purpose.

As we descended, we passed by ruined camps, identified only by collapsed ice walls left as haunting monuments to the storm's ferocity. I marveled at the number of birds I saw, frozen in midflight and catapulted into nearby ice walls where they remained imbedded. One still stood near a camp ruin, its feet and beak frozen into the snow as though feeding. We hadn't been the only ones caught off-guard.

I began to chuckle. "Hey Craig," I called back. "You've heard of mastodons being found frozen in glaciers with daisies still in their mouths?"

"Yeah?"

"Well, I think I understand how it could happen," I said, pointing to the bird. "A few more days of that storm and we could have been the ones discovered eons from now, frozen in ice with granola in ours."

"Better granola than retorts," added Randy. "If I found someone with a retort in their mouth, I'd think they had been suffering from some really strange disease."

"Copy that," yelled Craig. "Retorts SUCK!"

Our pace never allowed much time to appreciate what was an absolutely exquisite day. Thoughts of showers, beers, and good food egged us on down the mountain at what seemed to us to be blinding speed. In our present physical state, anything short of falling over would have been considered fast! By early evening, we had rambled to within a few hours of basecamp. With an angry sky poised over nearby peaks, Robert radioed ahead to alert the pilots to fly in and be ready to pluck us off the glacier.

In what seemed an eternity, we rounded the last bend and began trudging up the final 200 yards or so to the runway. The track carried us up a slight angle, almost an imperceptible one, but with knee-deep snow that clung to our boots and legs like cement, it was like wading upstream against a strong current. It took us almost one hour to walk the last 100 yards.

Pulled off to the side of the runway were two demolished planes. The first was sitting upright with a broken strut and one wing bent at a right angle, reaching toward the sky. We heard that it had gotten bogged down in the new snow while attempting an ill-advised landing and had ended up doing a 360 on that wing. The climbers and pilot had walked away with only a story to tell as evidence of their near disaster. The second plane was lying upside down, the result of a midair collision. Someone had flown into the air space illegally and was in the process of buzzing the airstrip when he collided with a bush pilot attempting to take off. Stupidity, apparently, had not been limited to the mountain. No one was killed, and the bush pilot had managed to maneuver his damaged plane back to Talkeetna.

We unloaded the sleds and packed our waiting duffels for the flight out. Vern, now quite bubbly with the prospect of heading home, listed our community food stores: four cans of tuna, a bag of crushed noodles, a pulverized box of Cheerios.

"Just give me a table with a view," I called out. "Oh, and make it a warm table."

The Cessnas dropped through One Shot Pass and came into view. It was a glorious sight. We held our collective breath and stood silently watching them drone up the glacier toward us. It was almost too good to be true. Framed among the towering peaks of rock and ice, they appeared tiny, fragile, and vulnerable as they hung in the air. Their final approach seemed to last forever.

"We've just journeyed to the edge and back," I said, embracing Craig.

He stood there, an arm draped around my shoulder, a tear running down his face.

During the flight back toward civilization, Cliff Hudson, clearly thrilled at our success, insisted on taking us flight-seeing over all the spectacular glacial and mountain formations in the area. Sitting next to him, I didn't have the heart to confess that all our team really wanted right now was to place our feet on dry ground and feel warm water cascading over grimy and frozen skin.

"You know, I've never seen anything like that storm you all survived in all my forty-three years in Alaska." Cliff's tone had grown a bit somber as we approached Talkeetna. "I'm just tickled ya'll made it."

"We are too, Cliff. Believe me, we are too," I yelled back over the roar of the engine.

A half dozen military helicopters lined one side of the runway near the hangars as we landed. They had two purposes and two purposes only—search and rescue, and body recovery. I got a very dull, sick feeling in my gut as I stared at the olive-green craft. Seeing them began to bring the horror of the last few weeks bubbling to the surface. I imagined the Koreans swinging beneath one of them, the Swiss guide and his last helicopter ride . . .

"Ruth Anne! There's a call for you." Cliff's son had jogged out onto the runway and opened the door even before Cliff had cut the engines. He pointed toward the office. "You can take it in there."

Bewildered, I hobbled quickly to the office and picked up the phone.

"Hello?"

There was a long pause as the person on the other end breathed in deeply. "Who is this?"

I recognized the voice through the static. "Bob? It's me, Ruth Anne. How did you know to call me here?"

"Oh my God . . . Ruthie, is that really you? I can't believe it, you're alive. I've been so scared I'd lost you," Bob's voice trembled and though I could not see it, I knew he was speaking through a flood of tears.

"Honey, they didn't tell you I was fine? We sent a message down the mountain a week ago." I supposed tears should have been rolling down my cheeks, too, but my emotional valve was stuck on off.

"No, no, they told me nothing. I've been calling every day and no one could give me any information. You should have been off that mountain a week ago. I was so afraid to hear the worst. It's been all over the news. Eight people have died so far, I think, many more injured badly. Are you sure you're okay?"

"Bob, I'm fine. A bit frozen here and there, but fine. You can't believe everything you hear in the news, babe. Yes, people died, but many others lived. We lived and, not only that, we summited!"

"You what?!"

"We summited."

"You're joking, right?"

"No joke, we made the summit—all of us, in one piece." As I spoke the words, the deed finally sank in. We had made it.

Against all odds we had stood on the summit. "I love you Bob! I've got to go and help the team unload. They're all waiting for me. I'll call you later?"

"I love you too. Summited! Hot dog! I'm so proud of you."

As I hung up, I turned and promptly ran into Cliff's son, literally. It was a small office.

"He's been calling several times daily for the last two weeks. A lot of the spouses and significant others have been calling. Everyone's worried sick. I don't mind telling you I'm looking forward to losing my role as the Disaster Control Central co-ordinator and going back to plain old air-service control."

He reached over and pulled a photo out of an envelope and shoved it at me. "Pretty amazing, don't you think?"

There, in living color, was a photo of the three Koreans dangling at the end of a cable beneath a military helicopter. I grimaced and shoved the photo back, wondering if I was ever going to get away from this stuff.

"Mind if I make one more call?"

He motioned to the phone and moved back against the wall. "Be my guest."

I called the Talkeetna Motel and discovered the three rooms we had begun the trip in were available. Seemed appropriate, so I booked them for the entire team. We unloaded the planes and then Cliff gave me a ride over.

As I stepped out of his truck, I was immediately mobbed by the girls who worked there and a few others I didn't even recognize. Taken aback, I just stood there stiffly and withstood the outpouring of affection as best as I could.

Sally led the outpouring of chatter: "Girl, your husband has been calling here every day since you left. He must really love you. We told him you were okay, of course, even though we didn't know if you were. We just hoped and prayed and lookie here, you've made it back. You should be so proud! Will you have a drink with us?"

"Thanks, but . . . well . . . I think I just want a shower right now." I felt speechless, confused. Too many people in too short a time pressing all around me.

"Of course. Of course, you must be so tired." Sally pressed her hands to the sides of my face and looked deeply into my eyes. "You come out when you're ready. We'll still be here, that's for sure."

I smiled and limped off, out the door and down the make-shift hallway, over the now familiar pile of clutter stacked near the door and into the sanctuary of my roomlet. Taking care not to bump my head as I had when I first arrived, I bent over slowly and unbuckled my boots. Layer by layer, I peeled off clothes that were quite probably beyond cleaning and fit only for purification by fire. My feet, now uncovered, revealed an interesting color combination of black, yellow, and pure white—the result of too many freezings and thawings. I stood and gazed at the figure that confronted me in the mirror beside the shower. Hair hung in strings from a face whose eyes appeared lost behind dark circles. Cheekbones stuck out sharply and peeling skin hung in layers from my bleeding lips and nose. Each rib was clearly visible, framing a stomach cavity that was concave and taut. My shoulders, elbows, and knees stood out, clearly defined and jutting prominently outward from formerly strong limbs now wasted away from the effort required to fight for my life without sufficient food. All of the hair had fallen from my arms and skin sloughed away from my legs in clumps. I gazed at the corpse standing in front of me, just happy to be alive when it appeared as though I should have died. It had taken a mountain only three short weeks to make me look worse than a *Life* magazine photo of starving and beaten war refugees. Only now did it become clear to me just how much I had laid on the line to make this summit. I had nothing left to give.

I stood under the stream of hot water for over an hour, alternatingly washing and standing, standing and washing. It took nearly a quarter of a bar of soap and a quarter of a bottle of shampoo to strip away the accumulation of three weeks' worth of body oil, grit, and grime. As I slipped into my travel pants and shirt, I felt nearly naked: their gauzelike weight was imperceptible compared to the thirty-five-pound heft and boardlike feel of the clothes I had lived in for nearly the last month. I kept staring at my feet, too, conscious of how small they appeared in street shoes compared to the Frankenstein look of my mountaineering boots.

When I stepped out of my room and into the "daylight" of an Alaskan night, it was almost eleven P.M. Despite the late hour and what most described as a "cool, crisp evening," the air felt almost tropical to me. A breeze wafted by and carried me with it to Maui—warm, gentle, and scented with the smells of spring vegetation. The moisture and humidity felt soothing to my raw lips and nose. The healing had begun. I left my jacket in my room, realizing quickly that it would soon become nothing more than extra baggage. The night would have been perfect had it not been for the arrival of mosquito squadrons, legendary even by Alaskan standards. I cursed, ducked, weaved, slapped, and staggered the few yards to the motel bar and relative sanctuary. Just before entering, I glanced up and in the direction of Denali. It was obscured by clouds, its visitors sealed behind a storm curtain that prevented any plane from flying into or out of base-camp. I had heard we were the last team to make it out ahead of the front that now pounded the mountain. Had we been only an hour later, we would have been stuck, hunkered down for another week of misery without food. Those climbers who had been frolicking in the warmth of the sun at 14,000 feet yesterday were hating life now, that was for sure.

Most of the team was already seated at a corner table, each picking at a plate full of food and swilling down tankards of brew. Liquid nutrition appeared to be the thing. I ordered a full salmon dinner, but when it arrived, I couldn't eat it. Despite all my elaborate food fantasies over the last few weeks, I no longer had the appetite to indulge them. It wasn't fair. My body had trained itself too well not to expect feedings. After a few attempts to shovel down food, I pushed the plate away in Win's direction. He smiled, nodded, and, without breaking his feeding rhythm, pushed away his now empty plate and began wolfing down the food on mine. At least the stress of the trip hadn't affected his appetite.

John, sitting next to a nearly full plate of something, seemed more intent on nursing a bottle of gin.

"You okay?" I placed my hand on his shoulder and squeezed.

He nodded yes, but his eyes blinked back tears. "Oh man. I phoned my wife ... took forever to get through. She thought I was dead. Everyone had been calling her offering condolences. We didn't even say much on the phone . . . just listened to each other cry."

John held up one hand and, with his thumb and forefinger barely an inch apart looked me right in the eye, a tear tracing a path down his cheek. "We came that close, you know?"

I nodded even though I didn't share his fear. We'd done everything by the book and within the appropriate margin of safety. Although there was no denying that Death had been on the mountain with us all, he never had any intention of inviting any one of our team into his tent—that I firmly believed. For a while, all that was heard at our table was the clink of silverware on china. Our team was lost in thought.

"You know, I'm honestly looking forward to simply waking up in the morning without frost feathers cascading down on my face," blurted Paul in an all-too-obvious attempt to change the mood.

Everyone stared at him, then Randy smiled. "Hell, I've lost so much weight on this trip I had to put a compression strap on my boxers just to get 'em to stay up."

Snickers and chuckles made their way around the table.

"Oh man, that's nothing," chimed in Franklin. "I've forgotten how to put my clothes on unless I'm lying flat on my back. Really. Got my clothes out of my suitcase and I couldn't remember how to put on my pants until I lay down on the bed."

"You're so full of shit! 'Course, I'm thinkin' of asking my wife if she'd mind my keeping a Nalgene bottle by the bed. Kinda got used to not having to walk anywhere to take a leak when I'm bedded down, you know," smirked John.

We had begun the passage back through the looking glass and into the land of reality and the living. Like Alice who escaped her Wonderland, we were going to be just fine.

⟨⟩

I found my seat on the plane, exhausted and relieved to be going home. In a few short hours, I'd be in Bob's arms again. I stared out the tiny window as I unwound the cord to my headset, preparing to escape the crowded world of the fuselage and the murmur of travelers too wired to sleep. I was tired and wanted nothing more to do except sleep. As I fluffed what little there was of the airline pillow, a man sat down next to me and stared.

I should have ignored him, closed my eyes, and gone to sleep. But no, I looked back, catching his gaze with mine.

"You were on the mountain, weren't you!" the man exclaimed.

Saying no would have been the smart thing to do, but then, my face had probably already given me away. "Yes," I responded wearily and reluctantly. And the floodgates opened.

The man said he had been the leader of an Austrian team who had weathered the storm at a lower elevation. For the next three and a half hours, he talked nonstop. As far as I can recall, I never said much more than "hmm" or "ooohhh" or offered the odd "Really?" I was the victim of a one-sided avalanche of information I didn't want.

"One climber fell into a crevasse near their camp when his harness broke. Rescued but just barely before he froze. . . ."

I just stared, trying to listen without really hearing, but that proved impossible.

"Knew the Swiss guide personally, a real shame. . . ."

The dark ooze of fear began to creep into my mind.

"Another climber removed his gloves to repair crampons and ended up losing both his thumbs to frostbite. . . ."

I checked my own blackened thumbs as he spoke. I couldn't believe it. The man was smiling. He was relaying the body count and parts assessment with all the glee and energy of a play-by-play sports announcer on TV.

"Saw a guy sledded through camp frozen solid right up the thighs. Never seen anything like it. . . ."

He must have seen our half-dead statistic we'd heard about. Though I was safe on a plane, I began to feel the icy cold fingers of the mountain tightening their grip on me again.

"Two Americans nearly died but were rescued at the last minute. . . ."

My stomach knotted as I felt a cold sweat break out on the back of my neck.

"Saw the Polish climber who froze his feet. He would lose both of them. . . ."

He was grinning while shaking his head in mock disbelief. My Austrian flight companion seemed to actually be reveling in reliving the tortures others had either lived through or succumbed to. It was as if he was measuring his survival as a badge of courage, made all the more magnificent by another's misery.

"A Korean staggered into basecamp carrying his comatose buddy who was injured from a fall when his rope broke. . . ."

I could take no more of this. Discreetly, I turned up the volume on the tape player and pretended to listen. I could see his mouth moving and nodded periodically, feigning interest.

Though I had made the summit, it was becoming apparent that this mountain of my dreams had laid claim to my soul. I had been to the edge, looked into the void, and stepped back. Now, more than ever, I needed to go home and flee the mountain.

EPILOGUE

Sometimes distance and time is the only way one can discover
peace and be allowed the opportunity to fully appreciate the
lessons learned from a traumatic experience. In my case, that
catharsis took several years. Even before my plane's wheels
touched down in a puff of smoke and screech of tire rubber, I
had embarked on what seemed to be a never-ending expedition
up an internal mountain of turmoil.

When I arrived home, I found I had escaped one storm only to
land squarely in the maelstrom of another. For some unknown
reason, I became a media darling. Local TV, radio, and print rang
me day and night, requesting interviews and photo ops. National
television news, including CNN, wanted live stories. The *LA
Times, People,* and others sent reporters and photographers to
cover what was becoming known as "my story of survival."

Even my friends were relentless with their quizzing and in-
quisitions. The more others asked questions of me, the more questions I asked of myself. What really happened to me on that
mountain? What did my experience mean to me . . . to others?
Did I actually learn anything other than suffering sucks and dying
is a permanent affliction best avoided if at all possible? Was the
summit worth the challenge? Would I ever climb again?

I began to get an inkling what it must have felt like to be a

Christian, thrown into a lion's den with only a short sword to defend oneself while hordes of screaming and bloodthirsty spectators looked on. Everyone wanted a personal account of the climb, something no one else had yet heard. No one from the media knew quite how to approach the subject: "Were you afraid?" "How much weight did you lose?" (twenty pounds). "Did you think you would die?" "Did you see any of the others fall?" "What was it like hearing their screams?" "Do you have photos of the bodies?" "Did you each bring your own body bag?" Many of the questions were downright inane!

A magazine reporter friend confided to me early on that a commonly accepted rule of writing among many in the field was: "Never allow the truth to get in the way of a good story." Having been so alerted, I assumed a guarded approach to interviews. Sensationalism was unnecessary in my opinion, since the bare facts, truthfully told, already defied description and pushed the boundaries of imagination. Still, as I progressed through the minefield of interviewers and questions, I soon discovered that my friend was correct. Even with the most careful dispensation of accurate information on my part, writers unfamiliar with the world of mountaineering frequently, and I hope unintentionally, created a distortion of fact.

An anchor woman quizzed me for a commentary piece running on the evening news. While her request to see my frostbitten toes caught me off guard, I thought nothing of it until I had slipped off my shoes.

"Get the toes!" she ordered the cameraman.

And there, in living color, my blackened and damaged toes became a focal point of a story that seemed to have more to do with damaged flesh than the actual climb. I had gone from mountaineer to Exhibit A, trapped in a sound-bite and color-photo hell.

I tried to avoid the news, but it was unavoidable. Everywhere I went, headlines screamed out at me from newspapers displayed prominently at grocery store checkout lines, gas stations, convenience stores . . . there was no escape. I learned of the deaths of the four Canadians, including the one whose boot I had repaired, from the news. I stared at the headline and felt sick to my stomach. On the way down from the summit, one had tripped and fallen, sweeping the others off their feet. Climbers below watched in horror as the four, probably too fatigued to save themselves after weathering the storm that swept through as we departed, tumbled 3,000 feet in a tangled mess of ropes, limbs, and colorful climbing garb. The mountain was obviously still hungry.

I tried to put on a brave front for the world, but things are seldom as they appear. While going through the motions of life, I secretly battled demons. An ancient Chinese curse, "May all your dreams come true," haunted me as my subconscious fed on a tortured mind. For months, I would awaken Bob as I leapt out of bed screaming, "Oh my God! They're dead, they're all dead." In a cold sweat, shaking, I'd stand and stare at him as he reached to offer comfort.

Even months after the climb, the storm still existed for me and hadn't yet been reduced to a mere story. Every talk show, every print interview, every slide show that some group asked me to present brought me screaming and kicking back to the mountain. On one hand, the tempest had become an abstraction. On the other, it raged on, still wrapping its icy tendrils around my heart.

Despite the cold chill Denali had left in my soul, I never once lost my desire to climb again, though I found myself wondering if I could physically manage it after all the frostbite damage I suffered. Then, of course, there was the little matter of all the panic around me from loved ones. I'd never be climbing again until they calmed down and put Denali behind them. Every time Bob read an article of the climb, or heard an interview, he began to cry. From family to friends, all shared a common mission—to keep me away from other summits at all costs.

Gradually, though, the physical healing process began. My damaged thumbs, feet, right leg, and face healed nicely. In 1993, I managed to gently broach the subject of my climbing again by proposing a 1994 expedition up Kilimanjaro to a group of women whom I had gotten interested in hiking. The idea was to share with everyone the exhilaration of a mountain climb with minimal risk. Bob even came along. The entire group summited and the challenge was sufficient enough that it gave everyone, including my beloved husband, a sense of real accomplishment and a very clear understanding of why people climb: Mountaineering can be great fun! Though still naturally concerned for my well-being, the safety net my friends and family had worked so hard to place around me was lifted.

After the success on Kilimanjaro and during another public appearance to speak on my Denali experiences, I began to find emotional healing. That others found and continued to find meaning in my nightmare made me take pause. Adventure becomes an abstraction unless grounded in reality and there needs to be something to come home to in order to share the lessons learned. As farfetched and amazing as some of the reactions by strangers and audiences were, they were unwittingly helping me discover value in the Denali experience.

What I realized is that I had left the mountain with a new appreciation for the human spirit. Denali hadn't taken anything from me and in fact had bestowed on me a gift—a new beginning and sense of connection with myself, with others, and with time. I felt an integral part of nature and all its elements. I had begun to feel whole and complete as never before, as if what happened to me on Denali was a necessary right of passage, a collection of lessons that would equip me for every day of the rest of my life. The more I talked about and shared my experiences, the more the layers of ice I had allowed to cloak my soul melted away. And, as the ice melted, the fire to climb began to burn again.

Because of Denali, I have come to understand fully the importance of establishing clear goals that lead to good choices and keep one from being caught on the wrong side of a judgment call. Why did we live when others died? Some might cite luck. I choose to point to all the decisions our leaders and we made as a team. We have no control over nature, that's a fact, but we do have complete control over the way we react to various situations that confront us each day. Every step up and down Denali can be likened to life. Each step we take is a step that deals with and manages risk. When measured against our own best effort, those steps can never lead to failure, even if a summit is not reached. It is the journey that really counts, and not a belief that one must arrive at the top at any cost. Those who cling to the belief that it is only the summit that matters often find themselves or their dreams crushed under the weight of the effort.

In looking back, I'm now convinced that we were never for

a moment alone on that mountain. That the storm was a passageway linking this world to another is a statement born of experience, not faith. Now, whenever my thoughts stray high onto the ice fields and snow of Denali, I head outside and stare into the inky blackness of night. There, while gazing at twinkling stars, I wonder if the only thing keeping me from somewhere up in the heavens is this body and earth's gravity. I used to challenge everything, demanding proof and justification for all things. Since being allowed to peer into a window of my soul that's normally shuttered from view, I no longer ask as many questions. I've come to accept that some things just are.

On April 1, 1997, no longer haunted by nightmares and itching to reach for the heights once more, I headed to Cho Oyu in Tibet—the seventh highest peak in the world (26,994) and a next-door neighbor to Everest. After spending a month doing carries and getting staged for a summit bid, I made a decision at 22,000 feet to turn back. The same storm that hit Everest and subsequently left five dead was now pounding neighboring Cho Oyu, and I had no desire to be trapped higher up in those deteriorating conditions. Denali had taught me well and my decision to turn around, even after a year of preparation and an intense desire to summit, was easily reached. Now home, I don't regret the decision for a minute.

I know that there will be other summits and many more adventures in my life. I also know that I belong in the mountains. They are a part of my existence and being.

In Memory of Those Who Died:

May 15, 1992

GIOVANNI CALCAGNO, age forty-eight,
fell from Cassin Ridge, body never recovered (Italian)

ROBERTO PIOMBO, age thirty, fell from Cassin Ridge (Italian)

May 17, 1992

ALEX VON BERGEN, age forty-two,
pulmonary and cerebral edema (Swiss)

May 20, 1992

SEONG-JONG JIN, age twenty-six, fell down Orient Express (Korean)

SOO YANG YUNG, age twenty-nine, fell down Orient Express (Korean)

SUNG TAK HONG, age twenty-five, fell down Orient Express (Korean)

May 21, 1992

TERRANCE (MUGS) STUMP, age forty-one, crevasse fall (American)

May 31, 1992

ALAIN PROULX, age thirty-eight,
fell 3,000 feet from the Messner Couloir (Canadian)

CHRISTIAN PROULX, age eighteen,
fell 3,000 feet from the Messner Couloir (Canadian)

ALAIN POTVIN, age thirty-eight,
fell 3,000 feet from the Messner Couloir (Canadian)

MAURICE GRANDCHAMP, age twenty-nine,
fell 3,000 feet from the Messner Couloir (Canadian)